The *RYA* Book of World Sailing Records

Peter Johnson

Adlard Coles Nautical
London

By the same author

Passage Racing
Ocean Racing and Offshore Yachts
Yachtsman's Guide to the Rating Rule
Boating Britain
The Guinness Book of Yachting Facts and Feats
The Guinness Guide to Sailing
Yachting World *Handbook*
Offshore Manual International
This is Fast Cruising
The Encyclopedia of Yachting
Whitbread Round the World 1973-93
Yacht Clubs of the World
Yacht Rating: 170 years of speed, success and
failure against competitors – and the clock

Published 2002 by Adlard Coles Nautical
an imprint of A & C Black Publishers Ltd
37 Soho Square, London W1D 3QZ
www.adlardcoles.co.uk

Copyright © Sir Peter Johnson Bt 2002

ISBN 0-7136-5903-3

A CIP catalogue record for this book is available from the
British Library.

Note: While all reasonable care has been taken in the
publication of this book, the publisher takes no responsibility
for the use of the methods or products described in the book.

A & C Black uses paper produced with elemental chlorine
free pulp, harvested from managed, sustainable forests.

Typeset in 10.5 on 13.5pt Concorde
Printed and bound in Great Britain by
The Cromwell Press, Trowbridge, Wiltshire

Contents

Preface iv

Photographic credits vi

1 • Anatomy of a record 1
From over the horizon appears a fast sailor

2 • How fast they really went 5
Early days and records: some of them questionable

3 • Flat out – mainly inshore 19
Observing and timing on smooth water

4 • Faster sailing offshore 37
Serious stuff: especially the north Atlantic

5 • More ocean routes 57
Many seas, many nations

6 • Around the planet 73
Authoritative words on circumnavigations

7 • Day's run 94
The continuing lure of the 24-hour distance

8 • Sailing firsts and other records 102
All kinds of yachting superlatives

9 • Power boat records 115
Propelled at considerable speed

10 • Records to go for 120
Here's what to try

Appendices:

1 Contacts and addresses 127

2 WSSRC ratified passage records 128

3 Ocean race records 130

Index of subjects 134

Index of boats and people 136

Preface

Sailing yacht speeds and times over a set course can today be measured quickly and accurately. It is remarkable how often records are being broken both in regular races and over individually attempted courses. These courses are both inshore on specifically flat water and offshore, sometimes over very long distances indeed. In this book, power boat records are also briefly described for comparison and interest, and ice and land yacht speeds receive just a mention. However, sailing records on the sea and other waters are now an important part of boating.

Certain conventions are used throughout these pages. Miles are always *nautical miles* unless stated to be statute (land) miles. Speed is in *knots* (one nautical mile per hour) unless otherwise stated. A dimension is almost always given with a boat name and this will be *LOA* (*length overall*) in feet then metres. Other dimensions, if given, will be stated, such as beam, draft or sail area.

Remember that the *average speed* for a passage must mean that at times the vessel was travelling considerably faster to make up for lighter periods. On long passages, there will even have been calms. No other speed searching vehicle actually stops involuntarily, as does a sailing vessel.

The name given alongside a boat is that of the owner or skipper. The yacht is not being sailed single-handed unless that is stated, even if words such as '…and crew…' are not always there. Unless single-handed, there are always at least two on board. Sometimes 'two-handed' is stated, but not necessarily. (This whole convention does not apply to the 500-metre run, including board sailors.)

Because this is a work of records and speeds, it is not possible to give extensive descriptions of who and what led to the design and building, or anecdotes about each vessel, desirable though they might be. There are a number of works of yachting history, collections about races and back numbers of yachting magazines for the reader who wishes to pursue such information.

Note that many of the records of all kinds have been broken in the last decade. Sailing vessels have become quicker in recent years for these reasons among others: computer assisted design, especially of multihulls, lighter (for strength of course) hull materials, materials which can take desired shapes in hull and rig, new sailcloth materials, electronic navigation to find the right weather, routeing from shore base, communications including knowledge of competitor whereabouts and performance, major financial input by sponsors and others (hence some strange boat names), and even the development of crew clothing for personal welfare and ability to keep going.

On occasion the toll at sea of men and boats is mentioned in these pages. The attempt to sail faster on oceans has not been without appreciable cost. There have been disappearances, deaths, men lost overboard, capsizes and founderings. However, it has not been possible to list all these when discussing a record or route, though sadly they have often occurred in previous or contemporary voyages of the record attempt. To turn round one of the clichés of the time, safety is not 'paramount'. Daring and danger are among the foundations of the sailing record breakers: which makes their glory all the more deserved.

Peter Johnson
2002

Photographic credits

1

Anatomy of a record

The world is full of records; the kind that are intended to be broken. They may be found on the inside pages of newspapers, on the internet and way down in the stories of the day on television news. You remember something like this: 'Ray Speedy and his crew of nine in the revolutionary 100ft trimaran *Tots Breakfast Food* were greeted by a naval frigate, local lifeboat and chartered fishing boats as the yacht sailed past Cape Clear early this morning to cross the finish line and break the Iceland to Ireland outright sailing record by more than 18 hours. Their amazing 73 hours 6 minutes and 33 seconds was achieved despite gales, calms and several hours repairing a damaged mainsail.'

Thus comes about yet another passage record achieved under sail – or does it? If it is to be taken seriously, a number of questions are posed. Who recognizes this achievement? Where is it noted and preserved? How do we know it actually took place? Did someone independently check the times? That name on the boat, *Tots* etc, is a sponsor surely and he will be announcing all the achievements to get his contracted bragging rights. Such news tends to arrive first but what is its validity?

Later if someone else achieves a better time, by what margin must it improve? Anyway, who cares? Where is the audience? After all, as with most competitive sailing, there is no stadium packed with an audience to clap and cheer the feat; maybe just those few vessels rolling in the ocean swell under a grey sky and a spot of Atlantic drizzle. One or two hands can just be seen waving as *Tots Breakfast Food* hits the prearranged bearing from a mark (or her GPS clicks on to the sought after figure); then she is away again, heading for harbour quite some way from the finish line (maybe off to Cork in this case). Across it, the sea continues to tumble gently, its small waves uninterested in their latest role. Such is the nature of this relatively lonely mode of breaking records.

At the heart of all this is the fact that water is the 'slow element'. Wheeled vehicles and aerospace vehicles go very fast indeed; so fast that in daily use they are run at practicable utilitarian speeds or 'cruising speeds'. But sailing vessels on water have always been slow in absolute terms: as a result they have simply been designed, built and navigated to proceed as fast as they can at any time. Thus there has invariably been keen interest in what speed can be achieved; but in recent years such speeds have been believably measured and reliably publicized.

In the pages which follow will be found the 'sport' or 'science' or 'hobby' of speed on the water (which of these will predominate?) chiefly under sail, but also under power. There will be a look at commercial and industrial aspects as well, for working ships do not necessarily run at maximum speed. But sail does.

The best speed might be for a few seconds, over a short distance or over a long distance. Logic seems to divide sailing records into sprints over a short given distance and then longer passages inevitably across open water. This is indeed what happens with the short distance speedsters in smooth water, but some sprints are achieved when on passage for the ocean goers.

Then there are conditions and criteria for setting records. A bizarre example might be 'the fastest non-European man and wife team in a wooden boat, with a hull colour other than white, less than 30ft and no engine, to cross from A to B between the months of September and March in the new millennium...' It goes without saying that this sort of achievement may well be true, but is so hedged about with conditions that it is of no interest to any possible competitor. It is extremely arbitrary. Having said that, it will be seen that most record set-ups are to some extent arbitrary; but the framework has to be reasonable. For instance, there have to be some acceptable groupings of types of vessel and other kinds of divisions.

We hear the announcement that X 'enters the record books...' What books are these? None actually, but such imaginary scrolls are beloved of tabloid reports. Possibly what the reader is meant to have in mind is that annual publication, which appears in many countries and in numerous languages, *The Guinness Book of Records* – or *World Records*. However, the publishers of that renowned title simply do not enter every feat which is brought to their attention. In any one year their listing of maritime, shipping and sailing superlatives is slender. There was a time when *Guinness*, under the editorship of Norris and Ross McWhirter, was strong on boating records of a selection of categories. However, with changed management, the footballers and pop stars have edged out the sailors. In the 1970s *Guinness* published some specialist volumes which included many records but, though authoritative, they were not annual, became unavailable and slowly dated. As for other 'books', records are scattered around in some specialized works (but beware outdating), back numbers of magazines and newspaper archives in paper and on websites. In this book guidance as to where sailing records can be found is given in the Appendix.

The speeds and times quoted here are for vessels floating on water. It has been mentioned that wheels are quicker: so are sand yachts cheats? Even faster are ice yachts, which can attain remarkable speeds on water – but the water is frozen solid and does not count. Most sailing and power records insist that the vessel must float when at rest and not be supported by dynamic lift only.

More and more, the 'sprint' type record attempt is held in purpose-made waterways or at least on carefully chosen stretches of water. The days of having a go on some reasonably convenient coastal site are long gone.

Of all the enquiries about records directed to yachting magazines and relevant organizations, the most common is: 'What is the smallest sailing yacht to have made the non-stop circumnavigation of the world?' Actually the query is unanswerable, but it is not without interest and there will be much more on this later.

In sailing, speed and times on passage are not the only superlatives bandied about. We hear about the 'smallest' for various passages and then there are the biggest, highest numbers and the earliest.

Actually earliest is a tricky one. It is closely related to 'firsts'. A 'first' is not necessarily a record. To take a simple A to B distance, the record time could be held by the first boat to have travelled it, while later attempts had slower times. Such claims and definitions will become clearer later in the book.

So far no figures have been mentioned, but there will be more than enough later! In sailing it is narrow band, the arithmetic being such that the chopping of many hours off the time of a long voyage only results in fractions of a knot better speed. Sailing times vary in the ocean from a few knots for older voyages, or specific 'conditional' ones, to late teens and early twenties, except in the most outstanding cases. Inshore there is a fixed speed result for the fastest sailing craft ever: we shall see how near to 50 knots this has become.

Under power hundreds of knots are grabbed by fiercely tuned up custom-built engines, but it is strange that under sail and power, the way to high speeds now involves being in touch with the water surface as little as possible. Flying, it has been said, is faster, so speed boats, sail and power, aim to achieve minimal mass and surface in/on the water, gained by foils, blades, planing surfaces and suchlike.

As in speed trials for all kinds of transport, prevailing weather conditions are a major factor. For an inshore run which actually takes a few minutes, challengers will find themselves waiting around for the 'right day' or 'right moment'. Out at sea, there will also have been planning, but in any passage lasting for more than a few days, the unexpected takes charge. Then whether a record occurs is partly up to the 'luck of the weather'. In other words, the most refined sailing machine will only break the previous record if the weather is at least as favourable as it was for the existing holder. So luck and good fortune both play their part.

A word here, in this world of institutions, lobbies and organizations, on who 'runs' sailing and power boating. About 110 nations have national authorities for sailing and yachting to which all their recognized clubs, classes and associations belong.

They in turn are members of the International Sailing Federation (ISAF), founded in 1906, with its headquarters in Southampton, England. The equivalent in the power boat world is the Union Internationale Motonautique (UIM), founded in 1921, with offices in Monaco. The United Nations' major maritime agency is IMCO (International Maritime Coordinating Organization), in London. However, sailing and power records are by nature based on enterprise and individuality; so at various stages and places, records may have been maintained on the initiative of just one person or perhaps a few members of a club or local association.

Let us leave this increasing complexity and fly back for an aerial shot of *Tots Breakfast Food*, her crew relaxing as she heads for port in a failing breeze. 'Lucky this wind at least held up as far as the finish,' say the crew. Of course they knew before they started what time they had to beat and when they must arrive. This was, as we have seen, achieved. But it is not for the skipper to announce success; nor is it for the navigator, or the crew. It is not for the sponsor to do so either, though he will surely go right ahead and run some ads which boost the sales of the famous breakfast food. On the contrary, there are a number of matters that might have gone wrong, beginning with the incorrect or disagreed timing of the start. Then there is a basic question as to whether this is indeed the same boat and crew that entered the challenge and started.

Before the attempt began, there were entries to be made and fees to be paid. Was any assistance given along the way, including offloading weight or onloading spares after a breakdown on board? And did the sailing boat ever use her motor or the power boat take on (if not permitted) extra fuel.

No: it was hard sailing, difficulties were overcome, and in due course, as will be set out later, *Tots Breakfast Food* is declared the record holder. After all that, was it worth it? Has money been made? Is there fame? Does it add to an existing roll of glory (for boat or for skipper)? Is the sponsor over-joyed? Or are boats more trouble than they are worth? Is it a step towards something else? Presumably it is some of these things or no one would ever have tried to set records.

As it is, sailors have been vying with each other in their quest for records for a very long time. Although more recent, the pursuit of records under power has been just as intense. So it is advisable to take a look at how they have all gone about this.

2

How fast they really went

'A sparrow hawk among the pigeons' was the description of the schooner *America* after her historic victory of 22 August 1851; after all, she had soundly beaten the finest yachts of the nation which ruled the waves. The important fact was that the British yachts of the Royal Yacht Squadron were left in her wake. But the actual speed is seldom, if ever, mentioned. In fact *America* took 10 hours 37 minutes to sail the course of 50 nautical miles, giving her an average speed of 4.7 knots. This was rather slow. Thus speed, as such, is not necessarily the standard by which racing yachts and their crews have been judged.

In the 2000 Olympic Games at Sydney, the Gold Medal winner in the Laser single-handed dinghy class purposely went 'slower' than the rest of the class in the last race of the series, in order to hold back his most dangerous opponent. No figure for his average speed is available because, of course, it would be of no interest at all.

Potential speed

The best time achieved by any sailing vessel, large or small, over a course between two points, is not necessarily related to the speed of her hull through the water. One yachting season some years ago, a survey was made of a number of weekend races to obtain data on the courses sailed. It was found that the winning yachts in each race had invariably sailed a shorter distance through the water (ie logged less mileage). This will be seen to be important in ocean records, but is not relevant to short inshore sprints. It would apply to racing around the buoys, but generally no one bothers to analyse that configuration.

In general terms, the longer a ship or boat is, the faster she is able to go.

A simple way of looking at this is that the vessel 'pushes out of the way' her own displacement each time she travels her own waterline length. So extra length for a given displacement gives higher potential speed. The assumption has to be made that there is the available driving force, either sail or power, to create the speed.

In the twentieth century, this rule has been eroded by the planing hull. It started with high power in small boats, which gave dynamic lift. Never mind the science of it in this work on records, but the hull was lifted out of displacement (at rest) mode, and speed out of all proportion to the size of boat resulted.

All kinds of development in hulls, engines, construction and other factors have flowed from that. The first such boats were called hydroplanes and appeared in c1907 in France; at 18ft (5.5m) they managed about 40 knots. In the 1920s, a few designers and builders of sailing racing dinghies pursued this idea in the International Fourteen Foot Class, by giving them V-bows and flat after-bodies. In a fresh breeze on a reach and if kept upright by the crew, such boats could also be persuaded to plane.

In commerce and war, sail or power, ships were load carriers and their displacement was inescapable. Only boats for sport could plane (with exceptions in due course such as high speed naval coastal craft). For displacement vessels there was, and still is, an accepted ratio of speed (V) against length on the load waterline, or rather the square root of the latter. This speed/length ratio is expressed as $V/\sqrt{L}$ which is expressed in knots (V) and feet (L) respectively. (It is not a metric convention, though it could be converted.)

In naval architecture, the application is for maximum speed, but there is no objection to quoting the ratio for averages or results over periods of time. So a 25ft LWL displacement boat, where this ratio is 1.6, would have a maximum speed of 8 knots. Yachtsmen know that this is fast sailing for a conventional hull of this size. Sometimes 1.4 is quoted as a likely maximum (equals 7 knots), but modern developments and sailing techniques (of which more later) enable these speeds to be exceeded.

In the nineteenth century, there was particular interest in the speed of two kinds of vessel. These were, first, sailing ships which carried market sensitive freight that needed to reach port before its competitors; and secondly, racing yachts, of which the largest would, by definition, be the fastest.

Sailing ship times and speeds

Clipper ships are famous for speed. They were created in the middle of the nineteenth century, and were smaller than bulk-carrying ships with improved lines for speed. They carried specialized cargo such as tea. However, large sailing ships other than clippers also had their share of record passages.

In these pages, the topic of how speeds and times are measured will often crop up. This arises immediately with the sailing ships of 150 to 100 years ago. Passages between ports or landfalls (not to the minute, but the nearest few hours) were not in dispute, but speeds for relatively short periods at sea were a different matter. These were based on the distance made in strong running conditions by these square riggers. As a heavy sea was probably prevailing, it was not ideal for taking accurate celestial sights. However, with such positions, distance run against time would give average speed for the period.

For 'almost instant' speed, a log would be run out, consisting of marks or knots on a reeled line. A sand glass would be started and the line stopped at the point the sand emptied. The mark on the line gave the (pre-worked) speed, the ship having sailed away from the line with a float on its end 'static' in the sea. That had obvious room for error. Yet another factor was that the master of the ship would want the best result for his own pride and for the owners to advertise their freight carrier. The resulting records are thus actually claims. Having said that, the speeds mentioned were those perceived as practicable and they have not been specifically challenged. It will be seen that when yachts first came to tackle records on the ocean in a systematic manner, the yachtsmen set out to improve on the sailing ship figures.

In his major work *The Search for Speed Under Sail 1700 to 1855* (Norton, New York and London, 1968), Howard I Chapelle states that long and intensive observation showed that the highest service speed usually recorded in a seagoing sailing vessel of good hull and rig design was in the neighbourhood of a speed/length ratio of 1.25 to 1.35. He gives as an example a waterline of 100 feet. The ratio of 1.25 then meant a speed of 12½ knots. This corresponded in practice with the American fishing-schooner racers *Bluenose* and *Puritan*, whose waterline lengths were slightly above the quoted LWL and 'which do not exceed 12 knots in competition'.

The best run over a 24-hour period was claimed as just under 19½ knots by the Black Ball liner *Champion of the Seas* in the Southern Ocean on passage from Liverpool, England, to Melbourne, Australia. It was derived from a distance run of 467 miles on 11/12 December 1854. A few years later in 1857, the clipper ship *Lightning* under Captain Enright covered 430 miles in a 24-hour period on 11/12 March. This averages just under 18 knots. *Lightning* is important in that she was a classic clipper built by the famous Donald McKay of Boston, Mass. Together with *Champion of the Seas*, *Donald McKay* and *James Baines*, she was built to the order of the

Notable sailing ship speed claims

DATE	SHIP NAME	DESCRIPTION	EVENT
1854	Champion of the Seas	Black Ball liner	19.5 knot average for 24 hours: 467 miles
1863	Thermopylae	Classic clipper ship	London to Melbourne 63 days
1864	Adelaide	Sailing ship freighter	New York to Liverpool 12 days 8 hours
1869-70	Patriarch	Scottish built clipper 1500 tons	London to Sydney record at 69 days. Sydney to London (via Cape Horn) 71 days
1870	Lightning	Donald McKay clipper LWL 218ft (66m)	430 miles in 24 hours
1875	Cutty Sark	Clipper, now preserved at Greenwich, London, LWL 200ft (61m) 2000 tons	Maximum claimed speed: 17.5 knots
1903	Preussen	Heavy (8000 tons) 433ft (132m) 5-master	17.5 knots during 4-hour watch

These sailing ships and clipper ships are well known to historians of the age of sail and were the starting point for yacht record attempts about 100 years later.

British Black Ball Line, and intended for the Liverpool–Melbourne route. Her waterline was 218ft (66m) and her displacement was 2084 tons. On this performance, the speed/length ratio mentioned above comes out at 1.2. *Lightning* was destroyed by fire in Melbourne in 1869; few of these vessels survived for many years. Clippers, in fact, were built light and were intended to make a good profit for the owners over a limited number of years.

A third claimed speed was by a much larger sailing cargo carrier, not a clipper at all; the five masted *Preussen*, 433ft (132m), and 8000 tons when fully loaded. A sustained speed of 17½ knots was claimed for a 4-hour watch period under Captain B Peterson in the South Pacific in 1903. So hers was a twentieth century record and must be viewed against the big cargo she carried and the big rig which drove her. She was an example of one of the last developments in regular commercial ocean-going sailing ships.

Sometimes quoted as the most reliable speed recorded is that of another McKay clipper, this time American: *Flying Cloud* of 225ft (69m) on a run from New York to San Francisco via Cape Horn (a regular route before the Panama Canal was built). Running north from Cape Horn up the coast of South America, her time and distance were checked carefully by the captain's rather mathematical wife, sitting below with three chronometers and books of tables. The distance was 374 miles and the time was 24 hours 19 minutes 4 seconds, which gave 15.4 knots. It is interesting that this is rather below the other claims mentioned. The whole passage took 90 days (6.45 knots).

Times between ports were much slower than over short distances because of inevitable headwinds and calms. Average speeds of the best clipper ships were more in the region of 6 knots for a voyage from Australia (wool) or China (tea) to England. *Cutty Sark*, the clipper now preserved on shore at Greenwich beside the River Thames, was 200ft (61m) on the waterline; 2000 tons displacement fully loaded. Her maximum claimed speed was 17½ knots; time in 1875 from Lizard Point, England, to Cape Otway, Australia, was 64 days. Her rival of the same size, *Thermopylae*, sailed from London to Melbourne, Australia, in 63 days in both 1868 and 1870. These times should be noted because the first attempts at individual records by yachts were to beat declared clipper times.

Thinking ahead along the same lines, here are some other sailing ship routes. *James Baines*, a McKay clipper, sailed from Liverpool to Melbourne and returned via Cape Horn (in other words a circumnavigation of the world) in 133 days, giving average speed of 8.9 knots. *Adelaide* made the transatlantic, New York to Liverpool passage in 1864, in 12 days 8 hours (12.8 knots). This was exceptional, having the benefit of the prevailing winds, and those presumably fresh or strong most of the way. It could never have been achieved east to west.

Such were the speeds and times of fast sailing vessels on the seas and the oceans as they stood and generally remained unrivalled throughout, say, the first half of the twentieth century.

Big cutters

Early yachts were contemporaneous with commerce being largely under sail (say about 1840 to 1880), so their speeds were comparable with the better speed/length ratios, probably around 1.3. Thus a good 65-footer could manage a maximum of 10 knots. The word 'yacht' comes from the sixteenth century Dutch *jaghen* meaning to hunt or chase; thence a *jaght schip* or *jaght* was a light swift vessel. Yacht came to mean a small sailing ship used for despatches, messages and government business, port to port, port to fleet or fleet to fleet. That is enough history except to say that it was but a short jump from conveying a government official to satisfying the leisure or business needs of the well-to-do. Whatever her purpose, speed has always been an essential quality of a yacht. Whether the speed of any particular yacht is impressive or not is another matter.

The success of the New York Yacht Club schooner *America* meant that there was a vogue for schooners in England for some decades after that, though the cutter remained the traditional English rig. In 1869 the French Emperor, Napoleon III, gave prizes for a race for yachts of all nations to be sailed from Cherbourg round the Nab lightship (off the eastern corner of the Isle of Wight) and back, a distance of 131 nautical miles. The six entries, all schooners, included British, French and one American, *Dauntless*. The race was won by *Guinevere*, 308 tons, taking 10 hours 17 minutes. The speed was 12.78 knots, but this was a large vessel, which would not look out of place alongside a clipper. The LWL is not recorded exactly, but a guess is 130ft (40m), giving a speed/length ratio of 1.1.

Fast forward now to the year 1893 when, for reasons that do not concern this book (but refer to *Yacht Rating* by the author for the story of the creation of this new Big Class), there was an unprecedented surge in the building of newly designed first-class racing cutters. The typical overall length of such yachts was between 120 and 130ft (37 and 40m). They carried huge single-masted rigs and were raced 'around the buoys' in estuaries, bays or up and down suitable shore lines. In the USA *Colonia*, *Jubilee*, *Navahoe*, *Pilgrim* and *Vigilant* were built, while *Calluna*, *Britannia* (for the Prince of Wales), *Satanita* and *Valkyrie II* were launched in Great Britain. The last was for Lord Dunraven, who used her to challenge for the America's Cup, losing to *Vigilant*. Of these nine huge cutters, Brooke Heckstall-Smith said in 1920: 'It was the greatest year in yachting history.'

These out and out racing yachts were fast by any sailing standards, with large crews doing everything for speed when required, and sitting along the windward rail at all other times. When racing, the yachts' slightly different sizes were compensated by time allowances.

Exactly how fast they sailed is not well documented, but the largest, *Satanita*, with an LWL of 93.5ft (28.5m), was timed on a measured mile in the Clyde estuary on a broad reach and in smooth water at 17 knots (speed/length ratio 1.5). There was no question of planing (a term unknown then anyway) and she simply pushed her bulk through the water, albeit on the sweet lines of a deep keel racing yacht. She was designed by J M Soper, had an LOA of 131.5ft (40.0m); displacement 126 tons and sail area just over 10000 square feet (937 square metres).

On 5 July 1894, on the Clyde, *Satanita* failed to bear away enough astern of *Valkyrie II*, where Lord Dunraven was on the helm, and smashed through her just aft of the mast. The latter sank in nine minutes, one of her crew being killed, but his Lordship and all the others escaped on to other vessels. Such was the power of these cutters.

The American *Navahoe* came to England in 1893, while *Valkyrie II* was at New York for the Cup. She raced around the buoys in the Solent against

Satanita, a racing cutter built in 1893 to the length and sail area rule of the time, had an LWL of 93.5ft (28.5m) and was timed at 17 knots on a broad reach.

Britannia and the others. One memorable course was from Cowes, around the Warner lightship, the Calshot lightship, then the East Lepe, twice round (these are all just buoys today); a distance of 50 nautical miles. The wind was said to be moderate NNW, and of course there was beating to windward and varying tidal streams. The time of the winner was 5 hours 46 minutes. The average speed was therefore 8.7 knots.

On 12 September 1893, there was a match race between *Britannia* and

11

Navahoe in the English Channel, for the Brenton Reef Cup (named after a shoal off Newport, RI). Though ocean racing as we know it simply did not exist, these two cutters were to race from the Needles rocks, 'lining the three main rocks up as a transit', to Cherbourg, where they would enter the outer harbour, sail behind the breakwater, come out of the other main entrance and race back to the start line. The distance was exactly 122 miles and there was a fresh easterly wind, which meant they only had to tack when passing through Cherbourg outer harbour. The remainder of the course was, with the effect of apparent wind, close reaching. It was reported that at one period on the outward leg the yachts 'were travelling upwards of 12 knots'.

The cutters finished at the Needles within one minute of each other, *Britannia*'s time being 10 hours 37 minutes 35 seconds; so they averaged 11.5 knots. This particular race, whose exact date in history is known, is well documented; the times are accurate and the tidal stream was about at right angles to the course. So here is a reliable speed for the big cutters of 1893. The waterline of 87ft (27.5m) gives a speed/length ratio of 1.2. It does make one wonder a little about the 17 knots quoted for *Satanita*.

American and British J-class inshore racing yachts off Newport, RI, in 1937. LOA was about 143ft (44m), but varied. Average speed made good to windward was 8 knots. The fastest of all was the US Ranger (sail number J5).

After the Big Class

There was sparse interest and little progress in speed under sail between 1914 and, say, 1950. The Big Class continued to race in Britain and America with added interest from yachts built to challenge and defend the America's Cup. Between the wars, this was sailed four times: in 1920, 1930, 1934 and 1937. The last three were sailed in J-class boats, which were designed to an American rating rule (the Universal Rule) and came out at about 140ft (42.7m) LOA and 87ft (26.5m) LWL. The purpose of such yachts was to race against one other; in other words to stay ahead of your single opponent on all points of sailing. Absolute maximum speed was not a priority, but speed to windward was (once you got ahead, then off the wind, it was relatively easy to 'cover').

The most advanced of all the J-class was *Ranger*, the American winning defender in 1937, owned and sailed by Harold S 'Mike' Vanderbilt. On 5 August 1937, she was timed on a dead to windward leg, the last one of the America's Cup match, taking 1 hour 14 minutes 45 seconds over exactly ten miles (the legs had to be exact under the rules of the contest) giving an average speed to windward of 8.01 knots. Her reaching speed is not recorded. If one assumes for this refined, but heavy, displacement yacht a speed/length ratio of 1.5, then the maximum reaching speed would be 13.95 knots.

Along with all other American J-class yachts, *Ranger* was broken up, but the British Js *Endeavour*, *Shamrock* and *Velsheda* remain restored in various ways to this day. I am not aware of any speed trials for one or other of them; like so many sailing yachts of all kinds, absolute speed is not their purpose.

To revert for a moment to the above J-class speed direct to windward (that is the direct resulting velocity mark to mark, not the vessel's speed through the water at any time), this is a record since such a feat is no longer considered worth noting. There are too many variables such as tacking speed and the tactical use of minor wind shifts.

What applies to the J-class fits racing yachts in general, or at least the established racing classes. Today there is more emphasis on downwind speed, which is, in effect, the potential maximum speed of the boat. Racing yachts are, however, subject to rules, which set bounds to their speed. These are for good reasons, the object being that yachts should be equal except for the skill of the crew and such development as is allowed, as well as maintenance such as 'polishing the bottom'. So one finds that the sail area is limited, the deck equipment must not be skimped, and anchors of at least a minimum weight must be carried. Many other 'slowing up' features could be listed – propellers for instance. Not only are these for equalizing

What is 'fast' in a sailing yacht?

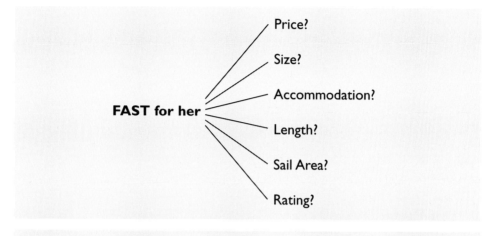

Travel on water is inherently slower than on land or in the air. The word 'fast', used too frequently, for yachts is relative. But relative to what?

competition, but also, depending on the type of yacht, for safety and seaworthiness. However, the latter are not necessarily conducive to speed.

For those with some knowledge of yacht and dinghy racing, this principle of 'slowing down' can be said to apply to all classes: keel boats (inshore racers), ocean racers, racing dinghies, multihulls, one-designs, restricted classes, formula classes, rated classes. Yes, there are exceptions and we shall meet them later.

Yet all or most racing yachts and even cruisers and dinghies are claimed to be 'fast'. It is an interesting word. It is of course a relative term: with fast tortoises and slow hares, everyone knows where to place the bet. In this book about records, the primary kind of figure is absolute speed. All attempts at such records are by fast boats. They are all fast. As for the 'ordinary' fast boat, her ability has to be contrasted with some other factor. She may be fast for her *price*; fast for her *size*; fast for her *extent of accommodation*; fast for her *displacement* (which is much the same as the last two); fast for her *length* (prestige and marina charges); fast for her *sail area* (price of rig and ease of handling); and lastly, which may for racing boats be the most immediate factor, fast for her *rating or handicap figure*. None of these has much to do with absolute speed, but one or more may be important to the owner and valid to quote. 'Fast' on its own is seldom much help.

Still imagining ourselves somewhere in the period between 1914 and 1950, the sport of ocean racing (in relatively small yachts) had arrived. The first Bermuda race was in 1923 (after a false start between 1906 and 1909) and the first Fastnet race in 1925. These races and others which grew from them were first sailed in heavy, seaworthy cruising yachts which really were very slow and not even very good to windward. Later some early speeds in such events will be mentioned, but only the occasional race result was anything other than quite slow.

The remaining type of potentially speedy (racing) boat, after round the buoys racers and ocean racers, was the racing dinghy or skiff or sailing canoe. The arrival of the planing dinghy has been mentioned briefly. This was first found in the Fourteen Foot Class, to which the word 'International' was added in 1928, when the class was recognized by the International Yacht Racing Union. Prior to that, it had existed in England since 1922 as a national class and before that in the guise of other 14ft dinghies which were raced (hardly 'racing dinghies'). From 1928, some similar boats in Canada and the USA were soon converted to the Fourteen rules and, of course, new boats built. The other tradition in these countries was the sailing canoe, which had been raced since the 1860s. This was a narrow, flat, scow type, kept upright by the helmsman (most types were single-handed) on a sliding seat.

Of course, both these classes were prone to the 'slowing down rule' syndrome just mentioned. But they attracted the best designers and builders, who did their utmost to increase speed within the rules, and being raced in relatively sheltered waters with rescue boats on hand, there was no need for the 'heavy seaworthiness' factor.

Uffa Fox was nothing if not innovative and in 1928 he designed, built and raced his Fourteen *Avenger*. That season in 57 starts she had 52 wins, two seconds and three thirds and famously he sailed her from Cowes, across the open English Channel (no escorts nor communications) to Le Havre and back. The outward passage of 110 miles took 27 hours which is 4.07 knots. This latter was an offshore speed with some light windward work, but the outstanding race record points to an undoubted breakthrough (a word not to be used lightly in these pages), because tactics and luck could not have notched up such a score. The actual speed through the water is not known and the existing boats were, as explained, 'slow'.

The boat had several profitable new ideas, but the main one was a V-bow and flat after section so that she could plane. Weight was also reduced as much as possible with the materials then available, though all these were heavy by today's standards. The boat is preserved today in the little Cowes maritime museum.

In the 1930s Uffa Fox made efforts to determine sailing speeds of sliding seat canoes, such as the one-man Gallant and, seen here, the two-man Brynhild.

From then on, racing dinghies followed the planing mode. The sailors began to say 'Wow, we must be going fast!' Then they wondered 'How fast?' Figures were bandied about. Few claims were made until about 1947, when increasing numbers of racing designs came on to the market each year.

Sailing canoe rules were different in England and the USA, so in 1933 Uffa designed and built two canoes to the American rules for himself and Roger de Quincey. They took these boats to the USA on a liner and won the principal cup, the International Canoe Trophy, as well as many other awards.

Following this campaign, the American and British rules were amalgamated into the International 10 square metre Canoe Class. Uffa designed and built one of the first of this new class, naming her *Gallant*. Frank Beken's photograph of Uffa on his sliding seat has become an icon of yachting history. The boat produced by the rule then was 17ft (5.2m) LOA and not much shorter on the waterline – narrow, with low freeboard and the essential sliding seat.

More important to us, Uffa spent several months trying to determine the actual speed of this boat, so different was she from all the one-design classes and other small sailing boats of the time. Eventually, on a fixed-shore measured distance (certified transits half a nautical mile apart) in the estuary above Cowes, he timed himself at 16.3 knots. Speed/length ratio was 4.0 and far beyond the conventional. Now here, if authentic – and who can tell after all these years – was absolute speed under sail as never before. It pointed the way to a different order of sailing speeds in small unconventional craft.

The International Canoe Class still thrives today after some 130 years, attracting the interest of about 300 enthusiasts and not much publicity. The narrow hull with its sliding seat is a one-design; the rig, still about 108 square feet (10 square metres), has some options. It achieves fast absolute speeds.

So much for the pointers to likely speeds and how they were attempted until about the 1950s, when the post-war expansion of sailing gave rise to yachts, dinghies and personalities which were to result in much more precision.

3

Flat out – mainly inshore

The shorter the distance a boat sails, the more chance there is of a high speed, but the more difficult it is to measure it. So the clipper ships turned in a much slower speed for a whole voyage (time easily noted) than a 24-hour run (time occasionally suspect). Similarly for modern yachts: time for a 10-mile leg was simply recorded (but unimpressive). Time for a sudden surge caused by wind and/or wave: well, what was it?

The word 'anecdotal' is overused, but it does describe the attributed speeds that were reported as new racing boats of all kinds appeared in the 1950s and 60s. One of the oft repeated speeds was that said to have been attained in 'secret' trials by the US Navy in 1956. There was actually a book around for some years, entitled *The 40-knot Sailboat*; its jacket showed a rather indistinct photograph of a multihull of some sort with spray flying from her. The story was that she was a hydrofoil-borne craft of LOA 30ft (9.1m) called *Monitor* 'developed' by Mr J G Baker of Wisconsin, Illinois, for trials by the US Navy. As the project formed part of a defence research programme, detailed data were not revealed, but speeds close to 40 knots were said to have been attained.

However, in October 1956 *Monitor* was reported to have been paced by a power boat at 30 knots; presumably the power boat had some form of speedometer. The hydrofoil craft was further said to have sailed at 'twice the speed of the wind' (though that is not unusual). As for the 40 knots, maybe that was the potential of the vessel or just a military secret. This rather shaky old story is recounted here, not only to demonstrate the kind of unsubstantiated claims around at the time, but to show the interest in sailing speeds which they stimulated.

Speed claims early on

'The 40 knot sailboat' was not the only claimant to improved absolute speed. Since before the turn of the century, open boats of 18ft (5.5m) and 22ft (6.7m) LOA had been developed in Sydney Harbour (Australia). Manned by huge crews, about seventeen in the 22-footer, the ballast was almost all human and movable and there was no ballast keel. On these 'skiffs' was a huge sail area set on excessively long spars. They raced inside the harbour and their successors still do so.

Exact speeds are unrecorded, but they flew past conventional sailing vessels. I have tried recently to obtain some sort of figure from the class but have met with no success. Maybe they just 'look fast'.

Both the hydrofoil experiment and skiffs had an important quality in common. It was a negative one and no less important because of that. Neither had to carry *weight* in the form of iron or lead keel (as a single-hulled yacht) nor in the form of cargo/payload (as in the commercial sailing vessel).

This was not any great revelation or invention. The elements of naval architecture were well known for hundreds of years. The problem was (and still is, though since solved in many ways) to design and build effective unballasted sailing craft.

Five modes

The third possibility, after foil lift and human ballast, is the multihull. The fourth mode can be said to be a combination of two of these, or all three.

The first (western, not Pacific) multihull is acknowledged as being a catamaran, *Experiment*, length not specified, but maybe about 50ft (15.2m) following two smaller prototypes, designed by Sir William Petty and built in Dublin in 1662. *Experiment* was later lost with all hands in the Bay of Biscay. A multihull may be a catamaran, a proa or a trimaran. A fifth mode is the sailboard. As with the other four, it will be discussed further.

In the late nineteenth century the American designer genius, Nathanael Herreshoff, produced several small inshore racing catamarans to circumvent rating rules. They immediately proved faster than their competitors and so were banned in their respective classes. They did not have to perform with any absolute speed, but just beat the other yachts.

Herreshoff was ahead of his time, but there was no big commercial future in this: he had enough conventional commissions anyway. It was left to the twentieth century for public promotion of multihulls and a notorious false start in the 1960s, when the Californian yacht designer and sailor Arthur Piver was quite successful in advertising offshore trimarans that could be built at moderate cost by amateurs.

These designs were claimed to sail very fast: figures such as 25 or 30 knots were suggested. A number of the designs were built around the world; some suffered capsizes, some had structural failure after amateur construction. An Australian, Hedley Nicol, enthused over the designs and developed his own version with more sail area, claiming yet better speeds. These two designers sailed their own boats offshore and even across oceans, but, sadly, both disappeared at sea in such boats.

Bigger multis

An Englishman, Derek Kelsall, built and sailed a Piver design, *Folatre*, in a 1964 Plymouth to Newport transatlantic race, but the vessel took the excruciatingly slow time of 61 days. As a result he became a designer himself. He changed the basics and in 1966 raced two-handed round Britain and Ireland (1950 miles) in his own creation, *Toria*, 37ft (11.3m), taking 11 days. Though thus averaging about 7.4 knots, he beat all other monos and multis in the event.

Eric Tabarly, the now legendary French sailor, took an interest in the Kelsall boat, had a trial sail and then went back to France and developed the theme with a French designer (of course), André Allègre. The result was *Pen Duick IV*, 67ft (20.4m), in which he and a crew made a number of voyages. One of his crew, Alain Colas, then acquired the yacht, renaming her *Manureva*. In the 1972 Plymouth to Newport single-handed event, he won in 20 days 13 hours, giving 5.6 knots, but it must be remembered that this is a windward race (current record 11.3 knots).

In 1973–74 Colas sailed *Manureva* around the world (starting and finishing at St Malo), with only one stop, in Sydney. His 168 days at sea gave an average speed of 7.34 knots; his best 24-hour run was claimed at 326 miles (13.5 knots). On a later voyage, Alain Colas and *Manureva* disappeared without trace in the Atlantic.

Completely independent of all the above multihulls (and rather earlier) was a development in Hawaii. A long-established ocean race was the Transpac; usual entries were very large traditional yachts and it was invariably a downwind trade wind reach and run from San Francisco to Honolulu. Rudy Choy built a 40ft (12.2m) catamaran, *Waikiki Surf*, for the 1955 race, finishing only just behind about four of the big monohulls (up to 150ft).

The next stage was a larger and improved version, the 46ft (14.0m) cat *Aikane*. She was what we would now call a cruising catamaran with high freeboard and spacious single deck between the two hulls. In the 1959 Transpac, this catamaran managed an average of 10 knots, beating the big schooners and ketches. On a cruise in the Pacific two years later, Rudy Choy claimed a 24-hour run of 306 miles. This average of 12.7 knots was no more accurate than the sailing ship distances of the nineteenth century, since electronic position finding was not yet installed in yachts. However, it was possible.

By the time offshore yacht design had left the 1970s, multihulls had shown consistent better speed than monos and were the winners in races which allowed both types, including the Plymouth to Newport transatlantic and the Round Britain and Ireland (with stops).

In 1978 Derek Kelsall designed the 56ft (17.1m) trimaran *Great Britain IV* as an outright offshore racer. Sailed by Chay Blyth and Rob James, she beat some 75 other yachts of all configurations in the Round Britain and Ireland that year, averaging 6.2 knots. The problem with average speed on this course is that it is beset with head winds, calms and the compulsory entry of stopping harbours. Even though time in port is deducted from the aggregate given, approaching harbours often results in failing wind.

Around this time the lead in fast multihulls offshore passed to French sailors and designers. Among reasons for this were that:

1 The *protégés* of the great Eric Tabarly were coming into their own;
2 The British races were being circumscribed by nervous organizing authorities with arbitrary limitations (first at 56ft then 60ft LOA), while the French ignored these and began to run their own events; and
3 There was a tragic toll of multihull sailors at sea, usually when single-handed on recent machines.

These casualties included Brian Cooke, Rob James, Mike McMullen and the total crew of a multihull which was pacing the 1979 Fastnet in a storm which claimed fifteen monohull sailors but no other complete boat and crew. French sailors were also lost including Colas, as mentioned, and Loïck Caradec. French multihulls started breaking the west to east transatlantic speed record in 1980, but this will be looked at in some detail later. By then the multi, in one form or another, was king of speed offshore.

Exact speeds inshore

Now let us get more specific, as was attempted in 1954 in the Solent. A strange four-sided course was arranged so that there was no beating, and

Early likely sailing boat speeds inshore

DATE	OCCASION	BOAT	SPEED
1954	Local trials, Cowes, IOW	Uffa Fox 18ft Jollyboat (heavy blown up 14ft int.)	10.23 knots on one leg
1955	Local trials, Cowes, IOW	*Endeavour* 18ft cat	14.6 knots by warship radar
1970	Yachting World, East Coast of England	Tornado Class cat (Class still active 2001)	16.4 knots across 355 metres by surveying instruments
1972	From this year, the 500-metre one-leg run was instituted by IYRU and RYA		

Some speeds recorded by rather crude methods. The deficiencies were known and timing methods were improved year by year.

the winner was a large 18ft (5.5m) version of a contemporary Uffa Fox planing dinghy, called a Jollyboat, sailed by an Olympic silver medallist, Charles Currey.

In July of that year a trial was repeated using shore-based measured mile transits. This time the Jollyboat was sailed by Peter Scott, who was President of the IYRU (later ISAF), and she recorded 10.23 one way and 6.84 the other way. This was declared an average of 8.54 knots which was somewhat meaningless. As for the organizers, they were enthusiasts of the yachting establishment, who today would be regarded as keen amateurs. The next year they obtained help from the naval guardship at Cowes Week and, by using HMS *Undine*'s radar, overcame the obvious wind direction constrictions of a shore-based transit. An 18ft (5.5m) one-off catamaran called *Endeavour*, sailed by Ken Pearce, was said to have managed 14.6 knots over about half of a nautical mile.

The accuracy of these figures was suspect, even at the time, and interest waned. There was one curious report in the mid-1960s that a 22ft (6.7m) British C-class catamaran called *Lady Helmsman* ('Little America's Cup' winner) had sailed at 30 knots. However, this was admitted to be the speed of a car pacing her along a seafront promenade. Hardly a recommended method!

In 1970 *Yachting World* magazine ran speed trials on an estuary on the east coast of England, in an effort to improve credibility. Sighting with some electronic survey instruments, they timed a Tornado class catamaran (still an Olympic class, incidentally) as covering 355 metres at 16.4 knots. This was becoming more interesting.

A fruitful and quite extensive discussion was reproduced in *Yachting World* in April 1970 between some authoritative figures of the time (most of whose names need no longer concern us) on the whole question of proper

23

inshore speed trials. Stripping away the inevitable false trails, the participants, guided mostly by Peter Scott (who had experience of speed trials in other fields such as gliding and coastal fighting ships), soon eliminated there-and-back, triangles, distances much over a kilometre and restrictions of various kinds such as not being allowed to use a canal. Most important, a well-sponsored exercise was envisaged with a money prize for best speed. Amazingly, possible speeds of 30, 40 and even 50 knots were bandied about.

The upshot of the meeting was support by both the national authority (RYA) and the international authority (IYRU) for a ten-day regatta at which entries would be able to make officially recorded best times over *a half kilometre (500 metres) course in one direction only*. Obviously the fastest angle to the wind would be chosen; therefore the course was within a circle. Yachts could then sail along any 500-metre diameter.

Exactly how the course was made accurate is now of little concern, since methods have long since moved on. The venue was Portland harbour, England, a wide, enclosed stretch of water where current and stream were negligible. That an effort was made is shown by the fact that half-kilometre wires were laid on the seabed by naval divers and buoys attached to the ends. Observers were stationed with stop watches; there were suitable communications and so on.

Probably the most important factor was that a tobacco company came forward as sponsor and offered a substantial cash prize for the fastest boat over the chosen ten-day period. This generated publicity and stimulated interest: a keen entry was assured.

A set of rules was required. The fact that these initial rules proved to have been sound, from this very first regatta, because the underlying principles have remained the same to this day (some 30 years later).

Apart from the 500-metre one-way run, they included: *yacht propelled by natural action of the wind; prior to and during the attempt yacht must accelerate from rest; at least one person on board, yacht must be in/on water (not ice or land)*. The corollaries of these are: no exclusive dynamic lift by towing on to the course area; no radio control to save any crew weight; no misunderstanding about ice yachts (whose speeds are mentioned elsewhere in these pages).

Of course, there were additional detailed rules at the time and which have been developed over the years.

One more essential piece of the jigsaw was an authority to run all this and maintain the rulings and records. What happened was that the IYRU authorized the project, but delegated the whole thing to the British national authority, the RYA. The RYA therefore, in due course, handled record

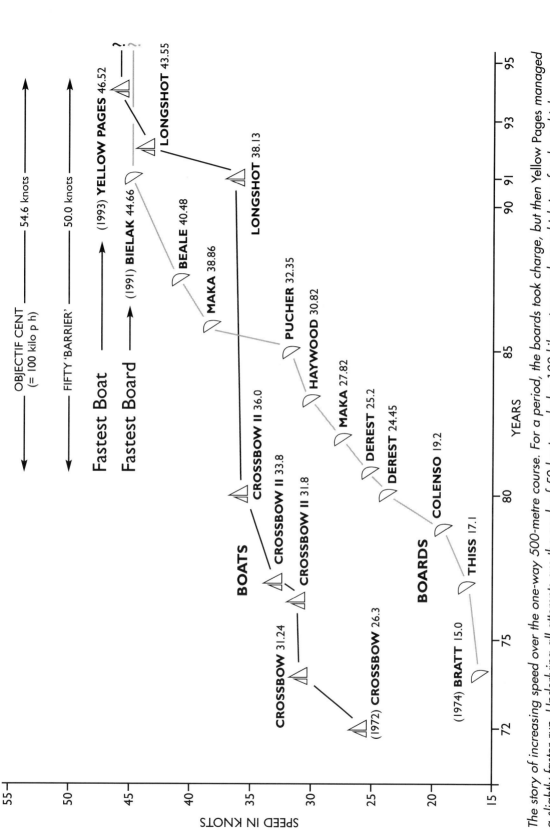

SPEED IN KNOTS

OBJECTIF CENT
(= 100 kilo p h) — 54.6 knots

FIFTY 'BARRIER' — 50.0 knots

Fastest Boat

Fastest Board

BOATS

BOARDS

CROSSBOW 31.24
(1972) CROSSBOW 26.3
CROSSBOW II 31.8
CROSSBOW II 33.8
CROSSBOW II 36.0
BIELAK 44.66 (1991)
YELLOW PAGES 46.52 (1993)

BEALE 40.48
MAKA 38.86
LONGSHOT 43.55
LONGSHOT 38.13
PUCHER 32.35
HAYWOOD 30.82
MAKA 27.82
DEREST 25.2
DEREST 24.45
COLENSO 19.2
THISS 17.1
(1974) BRATT 15.0

YEARS

72 75 80 85 90 91 93 95

The story of increasing speed over the one-way 500-metre course. For a period, the boards took charge, but then Yellow Pages managed a slightly faster run. Underlying all attempts are the goals of 50 knots and also 100 kilometres per hour which is a few knots higher.

attempts and speed course arrangements wherever they were in the world. For those who are stimulated by yachting politics, this system resulted in relief or grumbles, depending on points of view. Needless to say, as time went by, the RYA actually ran this through specific members of its staff and, to support them, a World Sailing Speed Record committee was created, including members from several nations.

Later the committee became the World Sailing Speed Record Council. In 1997, the Council left the umbrella of the RYA, appointed its own secretariat and office and thereafter reported direct to the international authority (ISAF).

First speed record holders

Return now to 1972, with the first Portland Speed Week, duly sponsored, about to begin. Tim Colman had a special boat built to a design by Rod Macalpine-Downie, a yacht designer of eclectic range. She was aimed only at the half-kilometre record in smooth water and nothing else. Named *Crossbow*, she was a 60ft (18.3m) proa, which could sail on starboard tack only. She had a span of 31.5ft (9.60m) with a 15ft (4.6m) pod on the end in which sat the crew of four; two of these ran up and down the span to adjust the angle of heel.

The best speed recorded by *Crossbow* was 26.3 knots on 6 October 1972; this was in a wind strength of 19 knots. So at last, after the claims, guesses and speculative sailing speeds of many decades, there was a properly measured speed under sail and an impressive one at that. This was an historic first.

Second fastest in 1972 was *Icarus*, owned by a syndicate headed by James Grogono and David Pelly. This was a Tornado catamaran with hydrofoils on each hull and one on the rudder: the speed recorded was 21.6 knots in the same wind strength. One other speed of interest, among the 18 craft that turned up for this first meeting, was a Flying Dutchman racing dinghy sailed by Olympic gold medallist Rodney Pattisson at 10.7 knots. Note that this 19ft 10in (6.0m) open dinghy was therefore close in recorded speed to the similarly sized Jollyboat of 18 years earlier.

Rather similar 'speed weeks' to that at Portland were held from time to time in other parts of the world. In the ten years following 1973, there were trials in the USA, Holland, Sweden, Germany, France and Australia. At Portland itself, the format remained much the same with small improvements and each year the hopefuls appeared. These varied from formidable machines which made runs close to the record, down to intriguing contraptions that never actually made it off the beach. In October 1973 (the

Outstanding among the early (1972) 'serious' recordings of inshore speeds over 'one-way' 500-metres, was Icarus, a Tornado catamaran with a foil on each hull and on the rudder.

second meeting), *Crossbow*, slightly modified, recorded 29.3 knots in a 20 knot wind. In September 1975, she came back again and managed 31.10 knots, again declared the world sailing speed record.

Staying with the *Crossbow* team, one sees Tim Colman appearing at Portland in 1976 with a totally new vessel by the same designer. *Crossbow II* was an 'asymmetric' catamaran; this describes two 60ft (18.3m) hulls with one slightly ahead of the other and a mast on each hull also staggered (again for speeding on one tack only). This vessel achieved 31.8 knots, and then in 1977 increased this to 33.8 knots. In 1980, after being on stand-by elsewhere in England, *Crossbow II* set a new sailing speed record of 36.0 knots. This was the highest she ever achieved. It was some years before the world record was challenged.

Sub speeds

In classes below the *Crossbows*, which were on a scale of their own, all sorts of useful (and useless) progress and experiments went on. One should not forget Christopher Hook, an inventor whose lifelong task was to convince others of what he called the 'hydrofin'. For years he had sought support from industry and defence circles for the power version of his craft, and marketed working models which were made by schoolboys in the 1940s. The principle was that there were 'feelers' on stalks ahead of the vessel which detected the oncoming waves and altered the angles of foils attached to the hull. However, when he brought a sailing version to Portland, it managed only 6.3 knots, because of the weight of the devices. For many boats, complication meant weight; the result was that sometimes a clever idea for increased speed was cancelled out by the weight of the same device.

Arising from the dominance of *Crossbow* and *Crossbow II* for these years, some other 'classes' were established in the mid-70s to encourage continued speed attempts by smaller/cheaper sailing boats. In addition to the outright world record, these were and are five in number, nominated by actual sail area. They remain today as follows:

- *10 square metres class* Anything up to and including 10sq m
- *A class* From 10sq m up to and including 150sq ft (13.93sq m)
- *B class* From 150sq ft up to and including 235sq ft (21.84sq m)
- *C class* From 235sq ft up to and including 300sq ft (27.88sq m)
- *D class* Over 300 sq ft

In all these classes there is also an all-woman crew category.

As mentioned, Portland Speed Week was sponsored by a tobacco company, but after providing invaluable support for five years, it withdrew. There followed several different sponsors and even a couple of years with no sponsor until 1986, when all sponsorship ended.

In 1975, a strange two-man sailboard was entered in the Portland speed week by Mike Todd and Clive Colenso. Regarded with some amusement, as sailboards (windsurfers) had not appeared before, its tandem crew clocked a respectable 13.5 knots. From then on, sailboards began to look quite serious in terms of speed. What was realized was that here was a craft of minimal weight, just floating enough to support one person (minimum crew under the speed rules); there was no complex gear (weight again) and no rudder to drag through the water. Two years later at Portland, a board – actually a then standard production Windglider (Dirk Thijs, Netherlands) – took the 10 square metre class record at 19.1 knots. Then in 1980 came a

Increase of board sailing speeds

DATE	PLACE	NAME	SPEED (knots)
1974	Portland	Reg Bratt	15.04
1977	Portland	Dirk Thijs	19.10
1980	Hawaii	Jaap van de Rest	24.63
1982	Portland	Pascal Maka	27.82
1985	Pt St Louis	Michael Pucher	32.35
1988	Saintes Maries	Erik Beale	40.48
1993	Saintes Maries	Thierry Bielak	45.32

Some of the outstanding speeds on sailboards/windsurfers. This table does not show every step up, but 20 years has seen huge development.

great leap. Off the island of Maui in Hawaii (where the board sailing and surfing freaks hung out), Jaap van de Rest (Netherlands) sailed a recognized 24.63 over the half-kilometre. The speed march of the board sailors had begun.

The result of this was that between 1980 and about 1993 the boards pushed all except highly organized one-off campaigns into the non-serious amateur class. In other words, the smaller boats (smaller than the *Crossbows*) were not going to beat the boards, be it with foils, fins, kites or anything else. Additionally, these were the days of a boom around the world in boards and the manufacturers gave major support to the speed stars using their particular boards.

Before looking at the progress of boards, a few speed results among 'the others' are notable. For instance, Nigel Irens, who in later years was a leading offshore multihull designer, sailed *Clifton Flasher*, which had five masts with what was virtually airplane wings over a foil-borne 27ft (8.2m) proa; this photogenic machine sailed at 22.14 knots in 1974. *Mayfly* was a consistent early foil boat with a conventional rig and was quite small: just 15ft (4.6m). The designer, Philip Hansford, improved this during a five-year period and ended with 23.0 knots in 1977. This was the A-class record until beaten by a tandem board in 1983.

Another type of speed attempt was, and still is, by the use of a kite. Yes, a grown-up version of the toy box kite, probably with numerous foils. This is floated to a height where there is a strong wind while the sea below is smooth; it also eliminates the heeling component which causes unwanted drag in ordinary rigs. It may even lift the boat slightly. A kite boat called *Jacob's Ladder* recorded 25.0 knots in 1982 and held the C-class record for six years. Many other interesting boats of widely different configurations turned up at Portland and elsewhere in these pioneering years. Only a few records were managed elsewhere: 'Brad' Bradfield's foil-borne *NF2* took the B class at Port Jefferson, USA, in 1975 for one year at 17.2 knots. He did it again at 23 knots in 1977 and a year later at 24.4 knots. Russell Long's *Longshot* recorded speeds up to 38.13 knots in 1990-91 sailing at different locations in Texas, and taking B and C class records. (These were not out-right, as by this time the boards had exceeded *Crossbow II*.)

Boards rule (for a time)

In the same year as van de Rest clocked his board record in Hawaii, he also visited Portland and produced the best speed at the meeting ahead of all other types of craft. Winds did not allow any records to fall, however, but a board was the fastest 'ship' for the first time. The next year a 'Sinker board' was again fastest at Portland; then in 1982, Pascal Maka (Fra) recorded 27.82 knots on a further specialist board, a world board and 10 square metre best. The specific boards at Portland and elsewhere were now being refined for the half-kilometre run and success was in the air.

Each year techniques and design improved:

* 1983 at Portland: Fred Haywood (USA) on a 'Maui special' sinker board; 30.83 knots breaking the '30 knot barrier'.
* 1985 at Port St Louis on the south coast of France in a wind (mistral) of 50 knots: Michael Pucher (Ger) on a special board; 32.35 knots, which incidentally beat the first *Crossbow*'s best.

A word about the half-kilometre course arrangements. It has been explained that in the early days, various configurations were tried before a circle was settled for, so that competitors could take any diameter depending on the wind. In places, and even at Portland, this was varied to a more or less fixed run in one alignment only. This was in the lee of a straight and accessible beach or piece of shore. The circle sounds useful in theory, but in practice at almost any location, there is only a narrow band of wind direction which allows flat enough water on the given course. In other words, most of the optional diameters on the circle are never attractive.

One stretch of beach ideal for speed attempts was, and still is, at Sotovento on Fuerteventura in the Canary Islands, where the persistent trade wind blows. With boards in the ascendancy, the depth of water along the shore became less of a problem, although it is bound to be an impor-tant consideration for foil-borne boats. At Sotovento, most boards can sail

Pascal Maka beats Crossbow II *on his board achieving 38.86 knots at Fuerteventura in 1986. For a number of years boards were the fastest craft under sail.*

within two metres of the shore line. A further step is to requisition even smoother water by sailing in a canal or trench. Its usable length is bound to be 500 metres, plus extensions for starting and finishing. This is exactly what was constructed near the shore at the village of Les Saintes Maries de la Mer on the Camargue coast of France between Marseille and Montpelier. It was on open ground so the wind blew uninterrupted, and there was the constant option of the sea itself a few paces away for practice or possibly a record attempt. It must also be remembered that now that speeds were in the region of 30 knots and more, only about 25 seconds were spent on the course provided.

In July 1986, on the Sotovento beach, Pascal Maka (Fra) made some twenty runs over 36 knots on a specifically designed board. The best of these was timed at 38.86 knots, which at last beat *Crossbow II*; so the outright world record was now held by a board.

World's fastest sailors (500 metres – current at the time of publication)

CATEGORY	BOAT	SAILOR	NAT	SPEED (knots)	YEAR
Outright fastest	*Yellow Pages*	Simon McKeon	AUS	46.52	1993
Board sq m	(Board)	Thierry Bielak	FRA	45.32	1993
On foils – A Class	*Longshot*	Russell Long	USA	43.55	1992
Women – any kind of boat	(Board)	Babeth Coquelle	FRA	40.05	1993

The fastest speeds in main inshore categories.

Trials then moved to Les Saintes Maries de la Mer trench. In all cases at this venue, specially prepared boards increased the outright record.

- 1988: Erik Beale (Gbr) sailed at 40.48 knots; this broke the '40 knot barrier' for any craft.
- 1990: Pascal Maka achieved 42.91 knots.
- 1991: Thierry Bielak (Fra) made 44.66 knots.
- April 1993: Bielak made 45.32 knots, again in Les Saintes Maries.

Eight years on this remains the 10 square metre record and, in effect, the sailboard record. It is not the outright record, however, for reasons about to be given, but it marked the high point of the boards in the record game.

The change of course configuration has been mentioned, but the methods of timing improved considerably over the same period. With the boards taking only about 22 seconds over the half-kilometre, the old stop watches were long gone. Videos of the craft are used. They must be identifiable (boards can look rather the same) with running digital time, synchronized between start and finish, and simultaneous view of transits or distance markers. Using such instrumentation, the speed is calculated to the nearest one hundredth of a knot. If there is a stream or current in any direction of more than one knot, the record is invalid; if it is less, it is measured and applied as a correction.

Fastest ever

For several years prior to 1993, an Australian team of yacht designers, comprising Lindsay Cunningham and others, worked on a totally original world sailing speed record vessel. During 1993, runs were made on the landlocked waterway, Shallow Inlet, Sandy Point, Victoria. Its size is difficult to describe, since there is no length as such. A cleanly constructed wingsail, height 37ft (11.3m), with a mast inside it, was supported just above the water on three splayed arms; each ending in a planing surface. Two are about 30ft out to port; one with the pod for a crew of two is at right angles to line of motion to starboard. This pod flies in optimum conditions. The boat was called *Yellow Pages* after the main sponsor. In October 1993, in 19 knots of wind, this speed machine recorded *46.52 knots*, as timed and ratified. The crew on board were Simon McKeon (Aus) and Tim Daddo (Aus). *At the time of writing (2002), this fastest speed ever recorded of a vessel, under sail and floating on water, remains unbeaten.*

It is not for want of trying since 1993, or indeed before, that this record has not been broken. *Yellow Pages* herself had many problems including one almost complete self-destruct before managing the record. She also holds the C class into which she fits, as well as B class (44.65 knots) when sailing with less sail area, and the women's C class (17.38 knots) with Jean Daddo (Aus). Still in 1993, with more sail area, she took the D class at 41.66 knots. This was beaten in 1997 by a speed of 42.12 clocked by *Techniques Avancées*, a 25ft (7.6m) wingsail foiler sailed by Navarin and Columbo (Fra) at Toulon.

Others have worked steadily in England, France and the USA since 1993 to break the barriers of *50 knots* (another 3.48 knots required) and/or

Yellow Pages – *the fastest sailing craft on water in the world (at the time of publication). Three widely spread planing surfaces bear her at up to 46.52 knots.*

100 kilometres per hour (=54.0 knots). At any one time, a number of projects are in hand, but at the time of writing (2002), here are some that have been known about for some time, or more recently revealed.

- *L'Hydroptère* (Fra), a large 50ft (15.2m) trimaran with foils on all three hulls. A further phase was launched in 2002 – a 'nouvelle version' – backed by the European Defence and Space Company, EADS. There was a budget of eighteen million francs. In charge of the attempt, Alain Thébault was hoping for 45 knots of speed in a 30–35 knot wind.
- *Objectif 100* (Fra), a canted rig foiler which has been more in the nature of a roll-over project for university students.
- *Techniques Avancées*, a proa foiler with a single wingsail on each hull.
- *Jellyfish Foiler* is trying for 100 kilometres per hour, as well as beating any current outright record. Sébastien François, in charge, was looking for funds. Her LOA was 18.4ft (5.6m), beam rather more; weight 330 pounds (150 kilos) and she was driven by a 107sq ft (10sq m) kite.
- *Sailrocket* (Gbr), with Malcolm Barnsley of the firm Aerolaminates (which deals with wind turbine blades), a proa foiler with single 235sq ft (21.8sq m) sail on canted rig: length 36ft (11m), beam 27ft (8.2m), weight 550 pounds (250 kilos).
- *Bootiful* (Gbr), a proposed 60ft (18.3m) catamaran with board type steering, which has been fiddled about with for years on the east coast of England.
- *Spirit Yacht* by Mick Newman (Gbr) who builds conventional boats under the same name. Apparently he has had a British government grant to progress a symmetrical canted wing mast proa with a single foil on the rudder.
- *Windjet* (Gbr) has been in hand since 1998 by Richard Jenkins in London. There is a single rigid fin balanced by a tail fin; projections for the 2002 launch are for three times the speed of a 20–25 knot wind.
- *Monofoil* is being progressed, so far by models, by an aeronautical engineer, Jon Howes (Gbr). Driven by a 'conventional' wingsail, cavitation is by-passed by the use of a single supporting foil only. The hull is a long crossbeam with the single skipper at the end of it.

Thus there is no lack of initiatives in the search for the utmost speed under sail. However, the proof of the pudding is in the eating (and in the timing and ratification), and numbers bandied about in respect of work in hand are numbers and not much else.

The highly respected *Yellow Pages* team worked on a new machine, introducing foils. Called *Macquarie Bank*, this looked hopeful, but ran into complex problems on the water (the very common cavitation and ventilation) so that an intended timing programme was abandoned. The latest news from this team was that a new tripod vessel, *Macquarie Innovations*, was expected to make new attempts from 2002. She has planing surfaces and not troublesome foils, is longer and wider, and has a low aspect rig. Though in theory 60 knots *was* feasible, control problems before that speed threatened to give a lower result.

Regattas for speed

The week or ten-day speed regatta still happens here and there, but it is no longer going to produce the world speed record. Those days are over because the special machine to beat *Yellow Pages* or any successor needs many weeks of stand-by and adjustment before the right day arrives for a feasible record attempt. So these examples mentioned above and others work away close to their chosen waters, or will be transported to a stretch of water in due course. The World Sailing Speed Record Council calls this a 'private event'. The organizer nominates a 28-day period and the WSSRC appoints a commissioner 'on call'. When the big day comes, the commissioner is called up and the timed runs are made. There are suitable fees and detailed rules for this.

There still exists the possibility of an 'open event'. This is a regatta-type happening, probably backed by a sponsor or a municipality. If world records are contemplated, WSSRC sends a commissioner for the period in return for due notification and a fee. The maximum for such an event is 10 days. For the reasons given above, such meetings are now rare. (If there are less than 25 boats, the event reverts to 'private' classification.)

The boards, as described, have been and gone; each serious '50-knotter' is engaged in a lengthy and singular operation and will perform when, perhaps after many weeks, the weather window arrives.

Gone are the old venues which included Sotovento, Les Saintes Maries, Brest (a major speed week for a number of years), and Tarifa, Spain, where single-handed Russell Long (USA) in *Longshot*, a catamaran on foils, challenged the boards in their heyday (1992) with 43.55 knots. This remains the fastest outright of any sort sailing on foils.

Portland, the original venue, limps on as a shadow of its former self, run by enthusiasm, but with no sponsorship, no financial backing and no hope of challenges to the world records. It simply times (with efficiency and accuracy) anyone who turns up. There is nothing wrong with that, but it is really no more than a pleasant week on the water for experimental craft.

As briefly mentioned, the World Sailing Speed Record Council

35

(WSSRC) is central to all today's attempts at new records anywhere in the world. Its operation is contained in its current rules, updated with minor changes from time to time. The core of its authority is the ratification, or otherwise, of any record. Until this is made official, any claim should have added the words 'subject to official ratification by ISAF/WSSRC'. A WSSRC-appointed commissioner must be present at the alleged record run and evidence is collected. In the classes (10 square metres etc), the sail area has to be checked by an official measurer immediately following the claimed record run. In order to claim a record, the new figure must be better than the old by a margin. The run should be made on the same course and with the same timing equipment in position to be equal to the accuracy of the equipment (so if this is 1/100th of a second, then the margin is 1/100th of a second). Where different courses are involved or the timing positions have moved, then the margin is 1/25th of a second. When there are transits afloat, the margin is 1 per cent. At the time of writing there is no additional fee for ratification on the half-kilometre course.

For a number of years, WSSRC has made available accepted records for another length of course: one nautical mile. This has not been subscribed to much, but is intended for offshore vessels that want to establish a speed over a short period of time, though it is open to any type. GPS positions are accepted for this single mile, and would be transmitted from the boat and recorded on shore without current input from the crew. Transits ashore, or buoys afloat, are also acceptable. The fact is, however, that the shorter the distance, the more likely it is that a higher speed will be recorded; thus the half-kilometre under sail continues to be the goal.

4

Faster sailing offshore

In the summer of 1987, strange stories began to appear in certain newspapers about a recent single-handed yacht voyage around the world. Until then, non-stop circumnavigations (see Chapter 5) could literally be counted on the fingers of one hand; so this achievement was surely of note. Furthermore, the time taken sounded as though it was a big improvement on earlier roundings. The figure of 129 days was mentioned, against the previous log of 150 days by Dodge Morgan in *American Promise* (see Chapter 6).

The sailor in question was 26-year-old Philippe Monnet (Fra). He started and finished at the port of Brest in the 77ft (23.5m) trimaran *Kriter Brut de Brut*. On her arrival on 19 April 1987, the sponsors, manufacturers of this excellent sparkling wine, declared the eponymous yacht had the latest record for *voyage sans étages*. Press releases and news duly circulated. A few weeks passed before tales or rumours started; the first from sources in New Zealand. People from the port of Bluff in the far south were surprised that the voyage was said to be non-stop. They distinctly remembered *Kriter* calling in there. The sponsors let it be known that the yacht had only anchored while Monnet had made some repairs without assistance. However, harbour officials at Bluff said that this was not what they remembered happening some months back. The sailor had come ashore, collected some necessary spares or other items and actually had a meal in a local hotel. A published photograph of Monnet sitting at a dining table was alleged to have been taken in the local hostelry. Thus the dispute raged.

This gave rise to a further piece of news that *Kriter* had also called at Cape Town, though the single-hander had not gone ashore. Lastly, came yet another story of some sort of assistance or contact in the Azores on the last leg of the voyage, but by that time the details were of little interest. The tangled controversy took various turns. These included:

'What constitutes a stop or a non-stop?'

'What is assistance?'

'What is single-handed?'

'Anyway, who is the judge in these matters?'

The bureaucracies of the national yachting authorities involved and the international authority (IYRU) exchanged letters and memos. The sponsors said this and that, as did experienced ocean sailors. The press revelled in daring on the high seas, falsity proved, press officers embarrassed and records besmirched!

Taking control

Somewhere among the yachting authorities, senior sailors, press and sponsors of other seagoing projects, it was pointed out that there did exist a body that handled sailing records; indeed it had done so in a systematic manner for some 15 years. Thus it was that the World Sailing Speed Record Council embraced ocean records in addition to the 500-metre run.

There was also a further 'political' factor. For nearly as long, a decade perhaps, I had compiled an annual information sheet for ocean racing authorities of best times achieved, records perhaps, in the world's principal ocean races: Newport–Bermuda, Fastnet, Sydney–Hobart and so on. Each year I issued this at the meeting of the Offshore Racing Council (ORC) that ran the world's then principal measurement and handicap rule and associated safety rules. But management and emphasis was changing there and it turned out to be exactly the right moment to ask ORC if this list and its originating committee (of one person – often the most efficient size) could move over from ORC to IYRU (the international authority), which in practice meant WSSRC. ORC readily acquiesced.

There was a third strand in this creation of a more practicable system. An author and sailor, Squadron-Leader D H 'Nobby' Clarke RAF (rtd), had for many years compiled record lists of different aspects of yachting. These embraced voyages of various kinds with feats and records, smallest, fastest, furthest and so on.

Nobby was well known as the person to ask about such facts. He wrote articles in the yachting magazines (1960s and 70s) and in particular was given a page or more in the annual *Guinness Book of Records*. Here selected records were published and the editors (Norris and Ross McWhirter) appeared to give Nobby a fairly free hand in this specialized field.

There was overlap with those offshore records of elapsed times which I had compiled and almost all figures and claimants appeared to agree. (If they did not it was often only necessary to wait until such an alleged record was broken and the new figure became available.) In a sense, therefore, Nobby's records, where relevant, became absorbed into the WSSRC list.

One could say, therefore, that it had a kick start. With IYRU (later ISAF) it has handled ocean passage records ever since.

As for *Kriter Brut de Brut*, the facts were acknowledged all round and if there was egg on anyone's face it was that of the sponsor's public relations outfit. Philippe Monnet, then in his late twenties, has gone on to achieve notable voyages since.

Before leaving Nobby Clarke, it should be mentioned that he kept all his records in longhand and corresponded in the same way. When anyone wanted some facts collected by him, Nobby quite reasonably charged a fee; one would then receive a neatly written and probably quite lengthy set of tabulations and supporting notes. All this worked quite well for many years, but as the feats and voyages of sailors and their categories quickly increased, it would appear that it all became too much.

One day Nobby, who was not getting any younger, announced he had given up and the project was ended. At least one American yachting magazine had the idea of buying his material and setting up a proper data base, but the negotiation came to nothing. It failed partly because of a combination of the fee demanded for the collection, and partly because of the idiosyncratic filing and listing, some of which – and all credit to the originator – was in Nobby's head anyway!

Within the offshore scene, WSSRC took on speeds (therefore times) only; it was never responsible for other records (earliest, oldest, etc), though these have impinged on its activities. I have continued to pay close attention to them and some were surely listed by Nobby Clarke.

Current record rules

Over the decade and a half for which it has been responsible for offshore records, the WSSRC has refined and extended its rules. With the authority of ISAF and its own moderate behaviour, it now has world acceptance, after some ups and downs in the early days.

One way it has extended opportunities is to have not just an outright record for each route but also a record for monohull only (assuming a multi holds the outright), one for all-women crew and one for single-handed. Combining these gives the following options:

- Any type of vessel, any number of crew
- Any type of vessel, single-handed
- Any type of vessel, all-women crew
- Any type of vessel, single-handed woman

- Monohull, any number of crew
- Monohull, single-handed
- Monohull, all-women crew
- Monohull, single-handed woman

There can be, and often is, a combination of these attained by one voyage. For instance, one-boat-one-trip may hold the monohull, the all-women and the single-handed woman.

It is an inherent option in record breaking of all kinds that there are *criteria*. By this is meant that one can set out conditional records, such as 'person living in southern hemisphere', 'two-person crew being married couple', 'only person with same dog on board for whole trip', and so on. However, WSSRC has fixed the variations as in the preceding paragraph.

As its name implies, WSSRC is international, so it does not register 'best time by a Russian', though it records the nationality of the record holder. If national bodies want to keep a count of their own nationals, that is a matter for them and indeed a sensible idea.

Another extension over the years has been the number of recognized routes, though these are strictly limited. If not, there could be a record 'from everywhere to everywhere'. If a local club or pub wants to give a prize for the best time from Yachtport to Leisuremouth (250 miles) that is just what it appears to be – local.

WSSRC has accepted routes which are 'established' or 'traditional' and the pages which follow will describe a number of them. In particular, for a given stretch of water or an ocean, there have to be certain limited ports, or maybe just one, at either side, which represent the record for the ocean. It is no good using other starting and finishing points, even if they create much the same distance, and then claiming a faster speed between them.

In outline, the boat, whatever her description, notifies the WSSRC that she will attempt a record on a recognized route. She is inspected to be identified for general compliance. Safety is her own responsibility. She is timed off, at a time of her choosing, by a commissioner (which is WSSRC jargon for an appointed observer). She is timed in at the destination, inspected and identified again. If the time is at least *one minute* better than the previous one, then the record is sent to WSSRC. If all is in order it is then ratified. The skipper receives an inscribed certificate, a permanent listing until the record is broken and any trophy which may happen to exist for that course.

The voyage just described is an 'individually attempted record'. A variation on this is a record obtained during an organized yacht race. There are hundreds of these, but, again, the well established, regular and traditional are the ones suitable for the list. The races must be from point to point and usually 250 miles or more, though a few very traditional shorter ones are included. Around the buoys, or races which vary their courses each time, are unsuitable. For these races, the WSSRC accepts the elapsed time recorded by the club or race organization.

The relationship between individual records and race established records over the same course is as follows. *If an individual record is better than the race record, then both stand, as individual and race respectively. If the time in the race is better, then it is both the race and individual record (with variations, of course, for single-handed, woman, etc).*

Here are some of the other offshore rules of the WSSRC:

- **The record itself** is the elapsed time in days, hours, minutes and seconds. The average speed in knots is computed, but is not the record.
- **The Racing Rules of Sailing** (as continuously authorized by ISAF) do not apply during individual record attempts.
- **Propulsion and sailing technique** Propulsion must be solely by natural forces. As with inshore, the vessel must float and support the crew at rest and must accelerate without assistance.
- **Single-handed** is an important definition and distinction. There is obviously one person on board, but if that person accepts any kind of assistance, then the voyage is no longer single-handed.
- **Assistance** During any attempted record passage, there can be no change of crew, nor can there be any outside assistance from sea or land. Stores and equipment cannot be taken on board, but the yacht can anchor or be beached and repaired by its own crew without any help.

  In the event of man overboard or other grave emergency, the engine can be started. The circumstances are then reported at the finish; as the time involved was probably 'wasted', allowances may be made. If another vessel or object (an oil rig, say) is fouled, then it is permitted for the crew of the other vessel or object to assist in getting the yacht clear. Generally these rules follow the practices of ocean racing and the customs of the sea.

  There are no restrictions on communication and information by all current technology, nor any restrictions on navigation systems. It used to be allowed for letters and mail to be taken off or dropped on board, but modern systems which contain e-mails, faxes and direct calls have, in practice, eliminated this.
- **Stops** Some specific courses do have 'stops'. In these cases, assistance in harbour or elsewhere is allowed, but the clock keeps

ticking away and the time is the total taken. In some recognized race courses there are specific stopping times, such as a wait in harbour of 48 hours. Then an aggregate of times on the course is taken.

- **Power under sail** As mentioned, the boat must be propelled by nature (wind, current, sliding down seas), but mechanical power can be used for charging batteries, pumping bilges, moving water ballast, canting movable keel configurations and boards. Power transmission can be used for handling sails and lines, but *not* stored power. This follows yacht racing convention, which calls for manual working of the boat 'on deck'.

- **The route** of individually attempted records generally follows the yacht racing 'string' analogy. A piece of string is pulled taut from A to B so that it comes up against land or unnavigable water. This gives the theoretical distance, usually rhumb line or great circle. The logged mileage on board is not considered by WSSRC. Where land or features are encountered in this way, they form part of the course and a boundary for the string.

    For an organized race course, there may be particular roundings and 'dog-legs' and these are inherent, so long as they remain the same over a period of years. It is realized that an established course can at some time change, but WSSRC would not handle a course that, while having the same name, changed its route on each occasion. A feature must be known to have been passed or rounded by the vessel, though it does not have to be sighted (ie, electronic means will inform the yacht that she has taken the pre-scribed route). No allowance is made for current and tidal stream, when record times are accepted.

- **Monohulls and multihulls** The distinction between them is duly defined from time to time.

Thus are set out the rules developed by WSSRC for ocean passages. However, these paragraphs are explanatory and also reflect the rules at the time of writing. *Any skipper, navigator or shore manager contemplating a record attempt must obtain the latest copy of the rules from WSSRC with any supporting amendments.*

Taking an interest

Ocean racing (in relatively small yachts) and also racing such yachts in regattas became popular after WWII. The big inshore classes were gone and keel boats (pure open racing boats with fixed keels such as the Dragon or 5.5-metre) were either local or on a rather select international circuit. Ocean racers they were, but they raced using rules of measurement and rating. From the rating of each boat was deduced a time allowance. In this particular field it remains the same today. But the important point here is that the winner was the boat with the best corrected time (it was/is actually called BCT) and not the first to finish. Some races did have prizes for the latter, but in these ocean races there were often extra prizes for a number of categories, sizes and achievements. In other words, the elapsed times of the race did not attract great attention. For a number of years after the war, world economics meant that many boats were either old or not very large; so the speeds were not examined too closely.

Most racers were smaller than the famous Sparkman & Stephens design, the 52ft (15.8m) *Dorade*, which is still sailing as a classic today. With her young American crew, in the 1930s she won the Bermuda race, the Fastnet and a transatlantic race – against both longer and shorter boats, of course, on time allowance. Her actual best day's run, however, was stated to have been 200 miles, an average of 8.3 knots (speed/length ratio: 0.87). The reason for this poor figure – and those of all the other ocean racers – was that the boat was designed to sail well for her rating and not in absolute terms. She was also intended to go faster (for her rating again) than her rivals in light winds, which tend to prevail when most summer racing takes place. So 'slowing her up' (and the others) for low rating was the result. The point is perhaps rather heavily made, but it explains the early lack of interest in speeds offshore.

When Colonel 'Blondie' Hasler came back from the war (and paddling canoes up enemy rivers to stick mines on anchored ships), he and a few others established the first single-handed transatlantic race from Plymouth, England, to Newport, RI, in 1960. One of his main ideas was to get away from these rules of rating, but actually what he had in mind was the development of easily sailed boats without crew. By definition though, the winner had to be the first boat to finish – no time allowances! He sailed a 25ft (7.6m) modified Folkboat. As we now know, it did not work out like that: the boats actually got bigger, then very big, and the winning time became rapidly faster.

This race, originally called the OSTAR, was one of the reasons for increasing interest in record times. Hasler's later creation, the two-man

Early days of offshore records: how they stood in 1974

COURSE	DISTANCE miles	YACHT	LOA ft	OWNER/SKIPPER	NAT	SPEED	DATE
Miami – Montego Bay	811	Windward Passage	73	Mark Johnson	USA	10.72	1971
Transpac	2225	Windward Passage	73	Mark Johnson	USA	10.02	1971
Ambrose Light – Lizard Point	2925	Atlantic	160	Charlie Barr	USA	10.01	1905
Newport – Bermuda	635	Ondine	80	Sumner A Long	USA	9.32	1974
Channel Race	225	Sorcery	61	J Baldwin	USA	8.71	1973
Sydney – Hobart	630	Helsal	73	T Fisher	AUS	8.56	1973
Bermuda – Plymouth	2870	Pen Duick VI	74	Eric Tabarly	FRA	8.20	1974
Fastnet	605	American Eagle	68	Ted Turner	USA	8.05	1971

About the time that inshore speed trials were becoming properly run, these were the fastest speeds known offshore. They were almost all very large American ocean racers; the specialized multihulls and short-handed flyers had not yet developed.

Round Britain and Ireland from Plymouth to Plymouth, had the same effect, though it had four compulsory 48-hour (or as specified) stops.

On the coasts of the USA, elapsed time took on a different look. Though the ocean races used time allowance, there was laid down a maximum size of yacht that was allowed to compete. For a number of years this was an LOA of 73ft (22.2m); such a boat became known as a 'maxi'. The maxi, then, was the first to finish and aimed to beat similar boats or the previous year's best time. So the maxis came to dominate any early lists of best times and can still be found in race records today, though exact maximum dimension rules have varied.

Next, these two aspects combined as the short handers found that they could sail boats of about, or close to, this size as well. Here are some boats holding race records in 1974, with year of record and speed: Bermuda race 1974, *Ondine* 80ft (24.1m), 9.32 knots; Bermuda to Plymouth 1974, *Pen Duick VI*, 74ft (22.5m), 8.2 knots; Los Angeles to Honolulu (transpacific) 1971, *Windward Passage*, 73ft (22.2m), 10.0 knots; Sydney to Hobart 1973, *Helsal*, 73ft (22.2m), 8.56 knots. Note that these were all 'recent'; speeds were beginning to improve in the mid-seventies.

The single-handed OSTAR (today called the Europe One Star), on a course from Plymouth to Newport, is westward against the prevailing winds of the northern North Atlantic and therefore a 'slow' race. In the initial race in 1960, Francis Chichester in *Gipsy Moth III*, 40ft (12.2m), won in 40 days 11 hours: that was 3.09 knots. In 1964, Eric Tabarly in *Pen Duick II* took 27 days 3 hours, 4.38 knots. In 1968 he leaped to the 70ft (21.3m) trimaran

Ostar – Europe One Star – Plymouth to Newport, RI

First ever race 1960	Gipsy Moth III	Francis Chichester	GBR	40ft mono	40d 11h	3.09 knots
Latest record 1988	Fleury Michon IX	Philippe Poupon	FRA	60ft multi	10d 9h	11.23 knots
Latest record 2000	Kingfisher	Ellen MacArthur	GBR	60ft mono	14d 23h	7.79 knots

The single-handed Plymouth, England to Newport, RI, is invariably largely to windward. Speeds show a limited increase, but at least passage times have more than halved.

Pen Duick IV and completed the race in 21 days 13 hours, 5.80 knots – that's better!

By 1984 interest in best times was established: Philippe Poupon in the 60ft (18.3m) trimaran *Fleury Michon* had the best time at 16 days 12 hours, 7.1 knots. Four years later, the same skipper slashed the time in *Fleury Michon IX* to 10 days 9 hours 15 minutes 19 seconds, 11.23 knots. The record stands to this day, despite three more of these races.

Note that, in the early years, the boats were getting bigger each year and changing to multihulls. Now multis are exclusively the serious contenders and built to the same maximum length under the rules of the event. As a result, further reductions in time depend on better design and techniques and/or suitable weather conditions at the chosen time of the event.

The classic route: North Atlantic eastward

The ocean battleground for the most developed racing yachts has been the North Atlantic and it existed well before OSTAR, which is discussed above. Races have been intermittent, for differing classes and from and to various ports. The latter though have been essentially from those between New York and Newport (includes New London, Gloucester) to England (mostly), Norway, Denmark, Germany or Spain. Historically most, but not all, have been from west to east because of the prevailing winds.

The 102ft (31.1m) schooner *America* on her way to the famous cup race in 1851, had cruised across from New York to Le Havre taking 20 days, a not untypical passage.

Although it is race records or non-records that fill the earlier years, the individual record is today on a fixed route between New York Harbor and Lizard Point, England; how this came about will be recounted later.

Back in 1866, the American civil war had just ended and yachts were once more being built in the yards. Attracting considerable attention was the 48ft (14.6m) *Alice*, built at Portsmouth, New Hampshire, which sailed from Boston, Massachusetts, to England in 19 days 7 hours, improving by two days the time taken by the schooner yacht *America* in 1851.

In October, three wealthy New York owners with newly built larger yachts, each declared his to be the fastest and challenged each other to a fitting match. The boats were: *Vesta*, 105ft (32.0m) centreboard schooner (launched in June), owner Pierre Lorillard; *Fleetwing*, 106ft (32.3m) schooner, George and Franklin Osgood; and *Henrietta*, 107ft (32.6m) schooner (built 1861 and ex-war service), James Gordon Bennett Jr, son of the owner of the *New York Herald*.

Each owner put in $30,000 (of course many times its present value), giving a stake of $90,000 to the winner. They were too impatient to wait until the following summer season. No, the race would be across the Atlantic Ocean to the Needles at the Isle of Wight, starting at Sandy Hook on 11 December 1866.

The yachts raced across the ocean in this mid-winter, and on 19 December six men were swept overboard from *Fleetwing*. There would be more casualties in this ocean from yachts racing others or records in the next 135 years. *Henrietta* reached the Needles in a gale after 13d 21h 45m; *Fleetwing* seven hours later and *Vesta* just 40 minutes after that – a unique Christmas Eve arrival.

One of the most lasting sailing ocean records of all time (1905 to 1980) is that of the American 185ft (56.4m) three-masted schooner *Atlantic*. Designed by William Gardner (also responsible for the Star class which still races in the Olympics), she was built by Townsend & Downey, Shooters Island, NY (builder of one of the Kaiser's racing yachts), and owned by Wilson Marshall. She was skippered by Charlie Barr (of America's Cup fame).

Atlantic was the winner of a race for a gold cup presented by Kaiser Wilhelm II and promoted by the Imperial German Yacht Club. It was to be from Sandy Hook, New York Harbor to Lizard Point, south-west England (and England's most southerly point).

Eleven yachts from Britain, Germany and the USA were started on 17 May 1905 by a cannon fired by the German naval attaché to the USA. The German cruiser *Pfeil* lay off the Lizard and timed in *Atlantic* at 12d 4h 1m. One reason for the choice of the Lizard was that the previously favoured Needles was felt by the Germans to be 'in the waters of the Royal Yacht Squadron' and they wanted to run the race entirely themselves.

Apparently *Atlantic* did go on as fast as possible to the Needles and recorded her own time. So it was that the Sandy Hook to Lizard route became the one to beat and to follow. (However, when the New York Yacht Club wanted to run a big boat and schooner race in 2002, it was able to quote the Needles finish as a precedent.)

In 1905 the three-masted schooner Atlantic achieved the transatlantic record of 12 days 4 hours 1 minute; not to be beaten for another 75 years.

As already explained, ocean races which followed were mostly not notable for elapsed times. The crack *Dorade*, in winning the 1931 race, took 17d 1h 14m (6.93 knots) from Newport, RI, to Plymouth, England. No one did any better in two more transatlantic races in 1935 and 1936.

In 1950, when boats were rather small, not long after the war, four British ocean racing yachts raced from Bermuda to Plymouth (2890 miles), after the completion of the Newport to Bermuda race. All were shorter than 40ft (12.2m) and with the long keels with rudders attached (no fins) that still prevailed. The 31ft (9.4m) sloop *Samuel Pepys*, skippered by Erroll Bruce, had the best time of 21d 4h 17m (5.69 knots). Adlard Coles racing *Cohoe*, 32ft (9.7m), was just five hours behind (and won on corrected time).

Jump now to 1977, with 'maxis' and large yachts around once again. That year, the American maxi *Ondine*, skippered by Pierre English, made the first serious attempt in modern times on *Atlantic*'s record. However, she gave up owing to light winds. English had been encouraged by a noted passage made in 1969, which had not been a record attempt. Jim Kilroy's maxi *Kialoa II* (USA) had crossed from Newport to Cork, Ireland (shorter than New York–Lizard) in 12d 5h 43m.

In September 1977, Chay Blyth and a crew of five made an attempt on *Atlantic*'s west to east figure in the Derek Kelsall designed trimaran *Great Britain III*, crossing in 13d 1h. In 1979, Alain Gliksman (Fra) and three crew set off in the trimaran *RTL-Timex* (ex-*Three Legs of Mann II*). Three days later, the boat broke up in mid-Atlantic. The four were nine days in a liferaft before being picked up by a Liberian oil tanker. Soon after came another trimaran, *Kriter IV*, with Olivier de Kersauson as skipper. The starboard float disintegrated at sea and all were taken off by the container ship *Atlantic Song*.

In a tragic repeat of the race of 1866, two American monohulls left New York on 29 December 1979. *Desperado*, 57ft (17.4m), was one and, within a week, had run into severe winter storms. The yacht was dismasted, the crew took to liferafts and were picked up by a container ship. The other yacht, *Shadow*, 50ft (15.2m), was heard to make a distress signal, but after that no trace of her or her crew was ever found.

The specific challenge

In 1980 all such attempts were put on a more specific basis. Two newspapers, *The Sunday Times* of London and *Le Point* of Paris, announced a prize of $50,000 for the first sailing boat to beat the 1905 record of *Atlantic* on her traditional route. Judging by recent efforts, these sponsors expected

Transatlantic classic route: progressive outright records

YEAR	YACHT	SKIPPER	NAT	TIME	KNOTS
1905	*Atlantic*	Charlie Barr	USA	12d 4h 1m	10.02
1980	*Paul Ricard*	Eric Tabarly	FRA	10d 5h 14m	11.93
1981	*Elf Aquitaine*	Marc Pajot	FRA	9d 10h 6m	12.94
1984	*Jet Services II*	Patrick Morvan	FRA	8d 16h 33m	14.03
1986	*Royale II*	Loïck Caradec	FRA	7d 21h 5m	15.47
1987	*Fleury Michon*	Philippe Poupon	FRA	7d 12h 50m	16.18
1988	*Jet Services V*	Serge Madec	FRA	7d 6h 30m	16.76
1990	*Jet Services V*	Serge Madec	FRA	6d 13h 3m	18.62
2001	*PlayStation*	Steve Fossett	USA	4d 17h 28m 6s	25.78

Steadily records were broken.

Transatlantic classic route: progressive monohull records

YEAR	YACHT	SKIPPER	NAT	TIME	KNOTS
1905	*Atlantic*	Charlie Barr	USA	12d 4h 1m	10.02
1981	*Kriter VIII*	Michel Malinovski	FRA	12d 3h 41m 33s	10.03
1993	*Winston*	Dennis Conner	USA	11d 18h 24m	11.21
1997	*Nicorette*	Ludde Ingvall	SWE	11d 13h 22m 5s	11.54
1998	*Mari Cha 3*	Robert Miller	GBR	8d 23h 59m 17s	13.54
2001	*Armor Lux*	Bernard Stamm	SUI	8d 20h 55m 35s	13.73

Meanwhile, monohulls struggled to improve on Atlantic's long standing record, but it eventually fell to them as well.

a long struggle and many stories for the papers over a period of time. Meanwhile, a reporter for them, Murray Sayle, had found *Atlantic*'s rotting hulk in a New England creek and some artefacts from the old yacht.

However all was cut short when, in August of the same year, Eric Tabarly and crew in the 46ft (14.0m) foil-assisted trimaran, *Paul Ricard*, slaughtered the record at an average speed of 11.93 knots and in the time of 10d 5h 14m. At last *Atlantic*'s record had fallen.

Once again Eric Tabarly had been a pioneer. Having shown that the 75-year-old record could be broken, he was followed by a succession of other multihulls; all were French, or perhaps one should say Breton. In 1981, Marc Pajot skippered the 63ft (19.2m) trimaran *Elf Aquitaine* in 9d 10h 6m (12.94 knots). The other records, as listed, were in 1984, 1986, 1987 and in 1988 when Serge Madec and crew in the catamaran *Jet Services V* crossed in 7d 6h 30m 24s (16.76 knots).

It was Paul Ricard, a 46ft (14m) foil assisted trimaran that at last broke the transatlantic record of Atlantic in 1980, sailed by Eric and Patrick Tabarly.

There is a trophy for the best time on this route originating in France and called the Loïck Caradec Trophy in memory of the sailor who skippered the 1986 record holder and who was subsequently lost at sea in a single-handed event. After the *Jet Services V* record, numerous attempts at improving on this remarkable time were made, but all came to naught. The main reason was that although a vessel usually started off on a suitable weather prediction and made good time, on approach to the British Isles, the wind weakened, so that either time expired or the time remaining was impossible to achieve.

However, *Atlantic* did retain at least one record: the best monohull. On return from the 1981 two-handed east to west transatlantic race, and in an informal course for French yachts, Michel Malinovski and a crew of four in the André Mauric designed 75ft (22.9m) monohull *Kriter VIII* just improved on the 1905 record by 19 minutes 46 seconds. Her time was 12d 3h 41m 33s (10.03 knots – one hundredth of a knot better).

In July 1993 (WSSRC had, by then, well established rules) the Royal Ocean Racing Club ran a west to east transatlantic race for monohulls (including contenders for Whitbread Round the World Race of that year). It started from off the World Trade Center in Manhattan and was to finish at Southampton on the south coast of England. The Whitbread 60 class 64ft (19.5m) *Winston*, skippered by Dennis Conner (USA), completed the course in 12d 8h 4m 12s. But this was not over the record route, although it was 'included'. *Winston*'s navigator declared that he had taken his own time at Lizard Point to give 11d 18h 24m and had therefore attained a new transatlantic record for monohulls.

The race committee time at Southampton gave no reason to doubt this, but there had been no independent timing at the Lizard and the claim could not be accepted. The start was also in the wrong place. Arrangements could have been made for the yachts to pass through the lines required and be observed, but this was not done. At least in 1905, there was a naval vessel to ensure the time of finish.

In April 1997, the monohull record on the proper course was soundly beaten by the 80ft (24.4m) 'maxi one-design' class *Nicorette*, skippered by Ludde Ingvall (Swe) and crew of 14 in 11d 13h 22m 5s (11.54 knots). In

Jet Services V *which, for at least 13 years, held the outright transatlantic record.*

Armor Lux, 60ft (18.3m), monohull transatlantic record holder, seen here crossing the Lizard finishing line in storm force winds in February 2001.

July that year, the recent winner of the 1996–97 single-handed Vendée Globe race, Christophe Auguin in the Open 60 *Geodis*, but with crew, claimed in the press to have beaten the monohull record by crossing in 9d 22h 59m 30s. However, the WSSRC had not been contacted, there was no timing in and no fee had been paid. In vain Auguin appealed to ISAF, but no record was confirmed.

In March the following year, the Italian Open 60 *Fila*, skippered by Giovanni Soldini (Ita), was looking as if she might beat *Nicorette*'s time by a good margin as she sped through the western approaches. Unfortunately, she capsized in stormy conditions, was dismasted and lost a crewman, adding yet another fatality to the transatlantic toll.

Later the same year, a very large yacht made the attempt. Again the weather was very bad indeed (October) and the newly designed and launched 147ft (44.7m) ketch, *Mari-Cha III* (Robert Miller, Gbr), crewed by Frenchmen and New Zealanders, swept past the Lizard with only scraps of

Right: The trimaran Primagaz *in which Laurent Bourgnon captured one of the most remarkable of ocean records, unbeaten since 1984: the single-handed transatlantic.*

sail and in 60 knot gales after just 8d 23h 59m 17s (13.54 knots). As will be seen, this was getting quite close to the outright (multihull) record and was faster than the Tabarly record which had broken the *Atlantic* spell.

The lesson from these voyages, and from some failed attempts and failed starts not mentioned here, has been that the North Atlantic is not to be easily defied in winter or even early spring and late autumn. Yet the best monohull so far (2001) did just that.

The Open 60 *Armor Lux* had retired at an early stage of the single-handed Vendée Globe race, which had started in November 2000. Her skipper Bernard Stamm (Swi) sailed to New York and added three crew. In the depths of winter (February 2001) he sailed the Ambrose to Lizard route in never less than 35 knots of wind, swept past the Lizard in 45 knots of wind and breaking seas and, although at 60ft (18.3m) less than half the length of *Mari-Cha III*, took the record at 8d 20h 55m 35s. This is a 13.73 knot average, and demonstrates the immense capability of the modern ocean racing yacht. During the passage, *Armor Lux* also took the 24-hour distance run record (Chapter 7) for a crewed monohull.

Single-handers have tended to go for the west to east route on their return from the OSTAR. The holder of that record scored a double in 1988 by taking the eastbound after winning the westbound: Philippe Poupon (Fra) in the trimaran *Fleury Michon IX* in 10d 9h 15m 19s (11.23 knots). The single-hander at the time of writing made a very fast time in 1994: Laurent Bourgnon (Fra) in the trimaran *Primagaz* in 7d 2h 34m 42s. During this voyage he also took the single-handed 24-hour distance run (Chapter 7).

The record for an all-women crew on the classic route is held by Tracy Edwards and crew (Gbr) in the 92ft (28.0m) *Royal & Sun Alliance* at 9d 11h 21m 55s (12.87 knots).

Start and finish

This important route has precision in relation to the start and finish line, as is the case in any yacht race. *Atlantic* and her fellow competitors started from the Sandy Hook lightvessel, but this has not existed for many years. The start line ever since the *Sunday Times/Le Point* challenge has been the Ambrose Light Tower. In 1998, the Tower was badly damaged by a ship and was then re-established a little further south. However, a plot showed that with a starting line running one mile south of the new Tower, there was negligible change in distance along the course to Lizard Point. Exact timing is invariably done by the New Jersey Pilots, who signal their figures to WSSRC.

Part of the entrance to New York Harbor

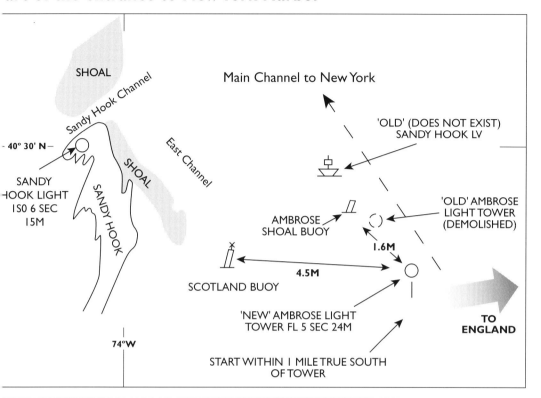

SHOAL

Sandy Hook Channel

Main Channel to New York

'OLD' (DOES NOT EXIST)
SANDY HOOK LV

— 40° 30' N —

SHOAL

East Channel

SANDY
HOOK LIGHT
ISO 6 SEC
15M

SANDY HOOK

AMBROSE
SHOAL BUOY

'OLD' AMBROSE
LIGHT TOWER
(DEMOLISHED)

1.6M

4.5M

SCOTLAND BUOY

'NEW' AMBROSE LIGHT
TOWER FL 5 SEC 24M

74°W

TO
ENGLAND

START WITHIN 1 MILE TRUE SOUTH
OF TOWER

Part of the entrance to New York Harbor, showing the start for the Ambrose Light to Lizard Point route. Although the line has altered slightly over 100 years, as the Sandy Hook LV was removed and then more recently the Ambrose Light Tower rebuilt further south-east, the sailing time changes in the direction of the finish are negligible.

The latter station their observer on Lizard Point. In the early days there was a Coastguard station there, which took the time, but it was disbanded. The observer is equipped with all usual modern aids of communication and timing. After passing the Lizard, the yacht comes to any convenient port for identification and checks.

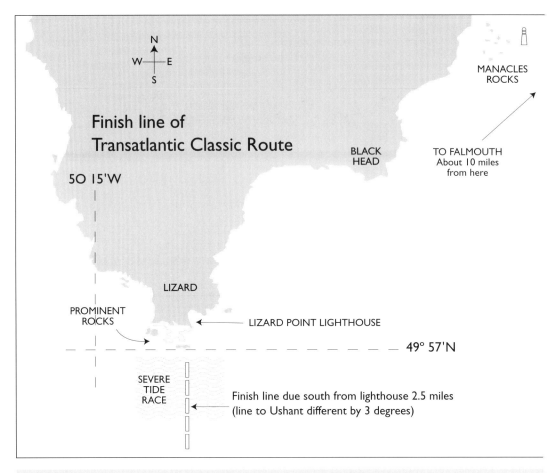

Finish for the Ambrose Light to Lizard Point route. The Lizard is the most southerly point on the mainland of Great Britain and also near the western extremity (see any chart or map). The WSSRC observer is positioned in front of the lighthouse with the line running true south from it. The rocks and tide race are potentially hazardous. The line for the Jules Verne Trophy (joining Lizard and Ushant) is 3 degrees difference, which is very slight at a couple of miles.

5

More ocean routes

The World Sailing Speed Record Council publishes its ocean passage records about once a year and they are also listed on a website. They show simply the latest record for each approved route, and the total varies from time to time. Currently there are about 120 sailing record holders.

The previous chapter focused on the North Atlantic classic west-to-east route and the single-handed east-to-west established race. In Chapter 6, circumnavigations of the world will be reviewed and some of the 120 record holders are looked at: those which are judged prominent, or of special note. But a record is a record, so readers should obtain and examine the current list.

Pacific Ocean

The first of these is the longest of all yacht record passages, other than round the world. It happens to be sailed in the Atlantic as much as the Pacific. It is also long established, because the nineteenth-century sailing ships used this route. The Panama Canal opened in 1914, so the sailing of any ship route from New York to San Francisco was via Cape Horn: 13,208 miles. The fastest commercial sailing ship time was by the 225ft (69m) McKay clipper, *Flying Cloud*, in a few hours less than 90 days.

The current holder dates from March 1998: an Open 60 *Aquitaine Innovations*, skippered by Yves Parlier (Fra), took 57d 3h 2m 45s (9.63 knots). This was actually in an event for the course called the Gold Race (because the gold prospectors took this route to California); but previously there had been individual attempts which included record holders and total failures.

Anne Liardet (Fra) and crew completed a slow voyage in the sloop *Finistère Bretagne*. Chay Blyth and crew in the 50ft (15.2m) Shuttleworth trimaran *Beefeater II* suffered a capsize 150 miles after passing the Horn, and were rescued by a passing ship after 19 hours in the water. Philippe

Success and incidents on the 'Gold Route':
New York – Cape Horn – San Francisco

DATE	VESSEL	TYPE	SKIPPER	NAT	RESULT
1854	Flying Cloud	Clipper Ship	Capt Cressy	USA	89d 21h
1983	Cystic Fibrosis Crusader	–	Michael Kane	USA	Rescued 120 miles NW of Cape Horn
1984	Beefeater II	Tri	Chay Blyth	GBR	Capsized, rescued near Cape Horn
1988	BNP Bank of The West	Mono	Guy Benardin	FRA	Foundered, single-hander rescued near Cape Horn
1989	BNP Bank of The West	–	Guy Benardin	FRA	Gave up on passage
1989	Thursday's Child	Mono 60ft 18.3m	Warren Luhrs	USA	80d 20h
1989	Finistère Bretagne	Tri	Anne Liardet	FRA	Completed, but took more time
1989	Elle & Vire	Tri	Philippe Monnet	FRA	Completed, but took more time
1989	Great American	Tri	Georgs Kolesnikovs	USA	76d 23m
1994	Ecureuil Poitou	Mono Open 60	Isabelle Autissier	FRA	62d 5h 55m
1998	Aquitaine Innovations	Mono Open 60	Yves Parlier	FRA	57d 3h 2m

There have been more failures than successes on the 'Gold Route', but these emphasize the achievements of yachts which have reached San Francisco over such a big distance.

Monnet was, unsurprisingly, involved in a dispute on whether he had sailed the course after dodging in and out of back waterways behind the Horn. In 1989, Warren Luhrs (USA) and two crew in the 60ft (18.3m) monohull *Thursday's Child* had to call in at Port Stanley, Falkland Islands, for repair during their voyage, but did reach San Francisco in a total of 81 days.

A few months later the Shuttleworth-designed 60ft (18.3m) trimaran *Great American* (USA) sailed the route in 77 days (7.55 knots).

After a well managed and fast passage on this difficult route, Isabelle Autissier (Fra) and crew held the individual record from February 1994 (until broken by Parlier) in the modified Open 60 *Ecureuil Poitou Charentes* of 63d 5h 55m (9.33 knots). This long ocean route through different weather systems, which cannot be avoided, is unlikely ever to show fast absolute speed.

Brief mention has been made of the Transpac race, which stimulated first to finish (line honours) attempts in early days. The old and present day course for this biennial event (odd years) is from Los Angeles to Honolulu, Hawaii. Special monohulls called ULDB (ultra light displacement boat) or 'sleds' have been built for many years in defiance of rating rules. The distance is 2224 miles and except for a short leg near the shore after the start, the course is invariably downwind in the fresh trade wind.

In July 1999, *Pyewacket*, 73ft (22.3m), owned by Roy Disney (USA), was first to finish in 7d 11h 41m 27s (12.38 knots). In July 1997, the 86ft (26.2m) catamaran *Explorer* was sailed by Bruno Peyron (Fra) as an unofficial entry and covered the route in the fastest ever time: 5d 9h 18m 26s (17.21 knots). This is among the half-dozen fastest ever passages under sail.

Other long distance races across parts of the Pacific and for which records are listed include:

- San Francisco to Kaneohe, Hawaii (Pacific Cup, biennial, even years)
- San Francisco to Hawaii, single-handed, 2120 miles
- Victoria, British Columbia, to Maui, Hawaii
- Melbourne to Osaka, Japan, two-handed event of 5480 miles.

Then there are races with records around the shores of the Pacific, as it were. Here are some of them.

In the long established and well supported Newport, CA to Ensenada, Mexico (125 miles), the best time (1998) was by *Stars and Stripes*, 60ft (18.3m), skipper Steve Fossett, in 6h 46m 40s, and resulted in 18.45 knots

Stars and Stripes, built for the 'freak' America's Cup of 1988, has, in the hands of record-breaking enthusiast Steve Fossett, recorded outstanding speeds in US races: for instance, an average 18.45 knots for Newport, CA, to Ensenada, Mexico.

which is the *highest average speed for the course recorded in any regular event in the world*. Steve Fossett had the boat (the unique America's Cup multihull defender) on loan from Dennis Conner, but Fossett also holds an outstanding number of records around the Pacific achieved in his 60ft (18.3m) trimaran *Lakota*: see list on page 64.

There are more Pacific rim races: San Diego to Puerto Vallarta; Long Beach to Cabo San Lucas; Swiftsure Classic (to the ocean and back from Vancouver); Brisbane, Australia to Nouméa; San Diego to Manzanillo. Then there is an infrequent race across the Pacific from Los Angeles to Osaka, Japan (5297 miles): the record for this is 32 days and it has not changed since 1994.

As for individual records across and around the Pacific Ocean, these are in the main a Steve Fossett/*Lakota* benefit! First there was a May 1996 4482-mile passage from San Francisco to Yokohama by *Lakota* with crew in 19d 15h 18m 9s (9.51 knots). Then Fossett came back single-handed to San Francisco in one leg, 20d 9h 52m 59s (9.24 knots). This was beaten by the crewed catamaran *Explorer*, as above, in August 1998 with Bruno Peyron and Skip Novak taking 14d 17h 22m 50s (12.56 knots). *Lakota*, crewed, sailed Honolulu to Yokohama, 3750 miles in August 1995 in 13d 20h 9m 22s (11.29 knots). These times seem to have sewn up the Pacific races and routes for a few years.

Mediterranean

The geography and summer weather of the Mediterranean are such that record courses are limited. However, there is one conspicuous one with the potential for very high average speed. This is a 458-mile run from Marseille, France, to Carthage, near modern Tunis, Tunisia, the site of the famous trading and military city founded in the ninth century BC. As a straight line course from the start at Pomegue lighthouse to the finish at Cape Carthage lighthouse, it offers the possibility of consistent speed from start to finish. There has to be a Mistral blowing to rush the yacht southward from the French coast.

Several recent attempts have failed to crack the 1991 holder, *Pierre 1er* (later *Lakota*) 60ft (18.3m) trimaran, Florence Arthaud (Fra), in 22h 9m 56s. This was an outstanding 20.66 knots. The monohull record was taken in 1998 by the giant 90ft (27.4m) all black *Stealth*, Giovanni Agnelli (Ita), in 1d 5h 2m 6s (15.77 knots).

There is a long established conventional ocean race called the Giraglia, which runs from St Tropez on the south coast of France (though ports may vary) round the rock of that name off Corsica. It is a kind of Med Fastnet, but about 240 to 290 miles depending on exact route. The current finish is at Genoa and the record is held by the 55ft (16.7m) yacht *Riviera di Rimini* at 1d 0h 11m 28s (10.34 knots). It will probably fall next time the weather allows.

This reminds one that race records are likely to stay unbroken for some years, sometimes for many years, in contrast to individual attempts. The latter generally sit tight at the place of intended departure and leave on a favourable forecast (for speed along the route). This may or may not turn out right. A race, on the other hand, starts on the hour and day appointed a year or more ahead. It is likely to set out in light weather or at least in conditions less favourable towards good elapsed time than when the existing record was set. The race is probably held every year, so the likelihood is assisted by numbers of yachts and 'compulsion' to set off. The individual attempt is a choice, which may well be put off or not taken up. Thus the Fastnet and Sydney to Hobart ocean races have important race elapsed time records, but on their courses no individual passage is any better.

Australasian courses

There are many well supported passage races, around and beyond the coasts of Australia and New Zealand and major islands nearby. These include the annual Sydney to Hobart race of 630 miles, Brisbane to Gladstone, Sydney (northward) to Gold Coast, Melbourne to Hobart, Brisbane to Nouméa, New Caledonia, and the Auckland–Fiji–Guam–Fukuoka of 5500 miles. The Sydney to Hobart, which always starts on Boxing Day (26 December), does not allow entries from multihulls; for many years from 1973 the best time remained at 3d 1h 32m (8.56 knots) by the Australian 73ft (22.3m) *Helsal*. The record set in 1999 is a vast speed increase and is held by *Mari-Cha III*, Robert Miller (Gbr), in 1d 18h 27m 10s (14.83 knots).

Atlantic coasts

Let us return now to points of departure and arrival on the coasts of western Europe, eastern USA, the Caribbean and the South Atlantic; the northern North Atlantic having been discussed in the previous chapter.

The trade wind routes may be thought the 'easy option' for passage-making and they are dependable, though modern sailors will try to find the best latitude for the season, as there is some variation north and south.

Several small boats have sailed between the French-speaking Dakar on the west coast of Africa and Guadeloupe in the Caribbean (2700 miles); only, of course, from east to west. A 19ft (5.8m) catamaran, the Dutch owned *Simac*, did this in 15d 2h (7.45 knots).

A more established race and individual route, mostly in the north-east trades, is from Cadiz, Spain, to San Salvador, also known as Watling Island, one of the places where Christopher Columbus is said to have first arrived. The distance is 3,884 miles.

In June 2000, as a qualifying sail for The Millennium Race, Grant Dalton (Nzl), Bruno Peyron (Fra) and crew in the 110ft (33.5m) *ClubMed* covered this route as an individual attempt in 10d 14h 54m (15.23 knots). The previous record by the much smaller *Jet Services V*, 75ft (22.9m), had stood since 1988, but now was beaten by about 5 days! There was a race organized from Spain on this course in 1992, 500 years after Columbus's epic voyage.

Other regular courses on the trade wind route are the Route du Rhum event, from St Malo to Guadeloupe, and the Jacques Vabre, Le Havre to Cartagina, Colombia. The course may vary. Open to multis and monos, best times get recorded and from time to time reduce. Closer to the Caribbean, a long standing course (811 miles) is Miami or Fort Lauderdale to Montego Bay, Jamaica.

Moving to the south-east trades, the Cape Town to Rio de Janeiro, Brazil, attracts a sizeable fleet down to quite small boats and multihulls, with conditions usually expected to be benign despite the long course of 3435 miles. The latest record in January 2000 was by the 75ft (22.9m) ULDB monohull *Zephyrus IV*, Bob McNeill (USA): 12d 16h 49m (11.27

Newport, RI, to Bermuda (635 miles)

EVENT/DATE	VESSEL	SKIPPER	NAT	TIME	SPEED
First Race* 1936	*Vamarie*	Vadim Makaroff	USA	4d 18h 50m 13s	5.53
Current Race Best time 1996	*Boomerang*	George Coumanataros	USA	2d 9h 31m 50s	11.04
Outright individual 2000	*PlayStation*	Steve Fossett	USA	1d 14h 35m 53s	16.45
Single-handed 1999	*Lakota*	Steve Fossett	USA	1d 16h 51m 54s	15.05
Monohull individual 1996	*CCPI Cray Valley*	J P Mouligne	USA/FRA	2d 5h 55m 58s	11.76

* Prior to 1936, Bermuda races were from ports other than Newport (New York, New London etc)

Current times and speeds over the Newport to Bermuda race, mother of all 'conventional' ocean races, together with the best time on the first race along the route.

knots). Another race to Rio, this time 1200 miles from Buenos Aires, Argentina, is a regular conventional ocean race with a current time of 4d 18h; there is no account of any individual attempt.

On the east coast of the United States there are numerous passage races and regular events, but some stand out as being significant in record terms. The classic is the Newport, RI, to Bermuda race; first sailed early in the twentieth century and long held biennially on even years. This has derivative, but quite separate, events including two-handed, single-handed and individual attempts: distance 635 miles. Unlike the other two 'old classics', the Fastnet and Sydney–Hobart, there is an outright individual and monohull individual, both of which are faster than the biennial race record.

PlayStation, then 105ft (32.0m), Steve Fossett (USA), has the outright record, sailed in mid-winter, January 2000, in 1d 14h 35m 53s (16.45 knots). The monohull record is retained by *CCP/Cray Valley*, 50ft (15.24m), Jean-Pierre Mouligne (Fra/USA), which in November 1996 took 2d 5h 55m 55s (11.76 knots). The race is in mid-summer on even years and in June 1996 the 78ft (23.77m) IMS racer *Boomerang*, George Coumanataros (USA), made the best ever race time in 2d 9h 31m 50s (11.04 knots).

A foremost course along the US coast, which can sometimes meet rough weather, is Annapolis to Newport, RI (473 miles), held on odd years; the record holder is *Chessie Racing*, 70ft (21.4m) monohull, George Collins (USA), in 1d 23h 45m (9.91 knots). From time to time there are races to Bermuda from Annapolis and from Daytona. There has been a race from Marblehead, Massachusetts, to Halifax, Nova Scotia (363 miles) since 1905: it is now biennial.

An individual course established by WSSRC is Miami to New York (947 miles). This has arisen because vessels trying prominent record routes sometimes cross from Europe to the Caribbean, then wish to sail to New York for the transatlantic route. On the way north from Miami a record might as well be tried. In 2001, Steve Fossett in *PlayStation* (USA), 125ft (38.1m) catamaran, sailed this in 2d 5h 55m 8s (17.57 knots) – unusually fast even among multihull records.

Although not in the Atlantic, passage records on the fresh water of the Great Lakes must be mentioned. The Chicago to Mackinac is the principal race. *Stars and Stripes*, 60ft (18.3m), sailed by Steve Fossett, covered the 293 miles in July 1998 in 18h 50m 32s (15.55 knots). *Pied Piper*, 67ft (18.5m), Dick Jennings (USA), holds the monohull record from 1987 at 11.3 knots. Port Huron to Mackinac (259 miles) is another regular race.

Records broken by Steve Fossett (USA)

Steve Fossett was born in 1944 in California, USA and now is based in Chicago, Illinois. He has pursued more ocean sailing records than any other individual. But his records also include other very adventurous sports as detailed below.

Sailing world records	miles	year
Miami–New York	947	2001
Yokohama–San Francisco	4525	1995
Yokohama–San Francisco, single-handed		1996
San Francisco–Yokohama		1996
Los Angeles–Honolulu	2225	1995
Honolulu–Yokohama	3365	1995
Round Britain and Ireland	1787	1994
Round Ireland	708	1993
Isle of Wight	50	1994

In races		
Chicago–Mackinac	372	1998
Newport, CA,–Ensenada	125	1998
Transpac, single-handed	2120	1998
San Diego–Puerto Vallarta	991	1998
Miami–Montego Bay	811	1999
Swiftsure Lightship course	137	1997
Long Beach–Cabo San Lucas	804	1995
San Francisco–Santa Cruz	67	1997

First places in distance races

12 events between 250 and 2225 miles
Airplanes 7 records
Automobile racing 5 places
Dogsled 1 record
Ballooning 3 distance, 8 altitude (USA)
2 round world attempts each covered over 12000 miles
Cycling 1 record
Swimming English Channel 1 transit
Cross country skiing completed 12 courses including 2 records
Mountain peaks 300 including 2 times on Everest

British Isles

Round Britain and Ireland

Blondie Hasler who, as mentioned, created the OSTAR, also began a regular event (every fourth year) round Britain and Ireland. The rules required a fixed total crew of two and four intermediate stops with fixed times in them; the distance is 1950 miles. *Toria*, the pioneer trimaran designed and sailed by Derek Kelsall, has already been mentioned. She took 11d 17h 23m in the first race in 1966. Speeds did not improve steadily, but fluctuated, eventually reaching a figure, in 1989, of 7d 7h 30m (10.40 knots) that has not been bettered. This was achieved by the 75ft (22.8m) *Saab Turbo*, François Boucher (Fra). The time is the aggregate of the time sailed between stops.

Today, though the two-man race continues, it is to some extent an old favourite, with the emphasis on 'old'. Multihulls and monohulls now sail around the islands without stopping and may be single-handed, two-handed or fully crewed. Champion of all is (once again) Steve Fossett (USA) and crew in the 60ft (18.3m) trimaran *Lakota*, which I timed out and back from a line at Ventnor, on the south coast of the Isle of Wight in October 1994. The yacht sailed 1787 miles anti-clockwise (the record attempt may be made in either direction) in 5d 21h 5m 27s, thus averaging 12.67 knots. The distance is less than the stopping race, as there are no diversions to and from ports. *Lakota* also holds the Round Ireland (the whole island only): 708 miles at 15.84 knots.

The recognized course around Britain and Ireland is invariably as follows: in either direction, around *all islands* including St Kilda, but excluding the Channel Islands and Rockall. (*Note*: Rockall is an isolated rock claimed by Britain far out in the Atlantic Ocean, and the Channel Islands have been Crown possessions since AD 1066, geographically adjoining the Continent and not the British Isles.)

In August 2000 the Royal Ocean Racing Club ran a non-stop race around Britain and Ireland which brought three new records. These were:

- Fastest monohull: *Sail That Dream*, 50ft (15.2m), Alex Thompson (Gbr), 10d 18h 27m 23s (6.91 knots)
- Any vessel in a race: the catamaran *Dazzler*, 50ft (15.2m), Mike Butterfield (Gbr), 10d 17h 2m 17s (6.95 knots)
- All-women crew, any vessel: the catamaran *Team Pindar*, 50ft (15.2m), Miranda Merron and Emma Richards (Gbr) (actually a two-person crew) 11d 6h 58m 17s (6.59 knots).

By coincidence, in the same month the single-handed record was established, there being no previous known completion. The yacht was *Zeal*, a monohull of 38ft (11.6m), Peter Keig (Gbr), 18d 13h 59m 59s (4.01 knots). He narrowly beat Sir Robin Knox-Johnston (Gbr), holder of many records, who was making an attempt in a boat of the same length at the same time and completed the course. Strangely that year, there were two other attempts: one gave up about half way and one was capsized and sunk, the lone sailor being rescued. It will be seen that all these times are far short of the outright record of *Lakota*.

Across the English Channel

When tabloid newspapers speak of the English Channel or 'the Channel', for instance in the case of swimming the Channel, they really mean Dover Strait, the narrowest stretch of water between England and France. This is often used for stunt crossings such as in a bathtub for charity; in the early days of aeronautics it was the focus of a first flight. Famously, the customs officer accosted Louis Bleriot who had landed in his aeroplane near Dover and reported, no aeroplane ever having previously come from abroad, 'I decided to treat him as for a yacht arrival...'

The WSSRC has a policy of not taking up proposals for record attempts across or near Dover Strait. This is because of the heavy traffic along and

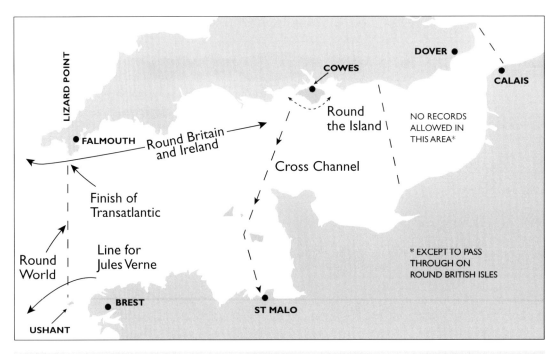

Chart of the waters between England and France, where a number of important record routes start, finish or pass through.

across and official objections from authorities on the coast of France. The established record route across the English Channel (in French *La Manche*) is from Cowes, Isle of Wight to St Malo, Brittany, 138 miles. This is also a long established race course of the RORC, so there can be a race record as well as an individual one. The exact race route can vary slightly, but the individual route permits simply the fastest course (there being islands and rocks along the way). In December 2001, the catamaran *PlayStation* (Steve Fossett, USA) broke all records on this route by taking 6h 21m 54s (21.68 knots).

Remember that it is 'easier' to sustain a high average over this distance, than over the usual minimum of about 250 miles for record passages, not to mention transocean routes.

By contrast the best speed in the annual Cowes to St Malo race is 10.98 knots by the trimaran *Spirit of England*, Peter Clutterbuck (Gbr) in July 1999.

Isle of Wight

There is an attraction in timing one's yacht around an island, be it Antigua, Robinson Crusoe island, Gotland or the Isle of Wight on the south coast of England. The last not only has a vast annual entry for its Island Sailing Club Round the Island Race, held since the 1930s, but was the winning course of the schooner *America* in 1851. Furthermore, a very large concentration of sailing yachts is stationed in several harbours within a few miles, often including the fastest and most recent designs.

In a way it is surprising that more attempts are not made on the records

Current times around the Isle of Wight (50 miles)

CATEGORY	DATE	YACHT	LOA ft/m	SKIPPER	NAT	TIME	SPEED
Outright	Nov 2001	*PlayStation*	125/38.1	Steve Fossett	USA	2h 33m 55s	19.53
Mono*	June 2001	*Leopard*	92/28	Mike Slade	GBR	4h 8m 55s	12.05
Mono	Sep 1993	*Dolphin & Youth*	60/18.3	Mat Humphries	GBR	4h 21m 56s	11.36
IACC (America's Cup Class)	On same		–	–	–	4h 23m 43s	11.39
Ultra 30	occasion as *Leopard*	First in Class	–	–	–	4h 26m 22s	11.26
Etchells F22	above		–	–	–	6h 35m 19s	7.59
Sonar OD			–	–	–	7h 26m 55s	6.71

* Powered sail handling

Though this is a short course for distance (50 miles) among the ocean records, the route is long established and easily accessible to many yachting harbours. The 'circular' course and the tidal streams make improving times a chancy matter. In this table some times of 'ordinary boats' noted on the same day as the records are shown for comparison.

around the island, but tidal and wind conditions are seldom 'right'. For instance, if a fair tidal stream is taken around three sides of its diamond shape, then the fourth will be foul. The same goes for wind direction, though there is always the chance of a favourable change. Boats of various types have sometimes waited many weeks to make an attempt. The outright time for this 50-mile sprint is held by Steve Fossett in *PlayStation* in November 2001 in 2h 33m 55s (19.53 knots). The record in the annual race is held by *Dexia Eure et Loire* and was in June 2001. She took 3h 10m 11s (15.77 knots) with an Anglo-French crew (Rodney Pattisson and Francis Joyon).

Fastnet race

The Fastnet race run biennially in early August by the RORC is from Cowes, Isle of Wight, westward to Fastnet Rock off south-west Ireland, thence to the finish at Plymouth, south-west England, distance 605 miles. Its progressive best times and speeds are instructive because the race, first held in 1925, has invariably attracted the latest ocean racers; the times were always taken accurately and it has an international entry. The weather can be anything from prolonged calms and light air to successive severe gales.

The best time at the finish of any yacht in any Fastnet was in that first race on 21 August 1925, by the Havre Pilot Cutter yacht *Jolie Brise* (Gbr), 48ft (14.6m), with 6d 2h 45m (4.26 knots) on a very slightly longer course.

For reasons previously explained (weather and rating considerations), best elapsed time will seldom improve in successive races. In 1928, the 55ft (16.8m) schooner *Nina* (USA), which had been designed for a transatlantic

Fastnet race (605 miles)

DATE	YACHT	LOA ft/m	OWNER	NAT	TIME	SPEED
1925	Jolie Brise	48/14.6	George Martin	GBR	6d 2h 45m	4.26
1928	Nina	55/16.8	Sherman Hoyt	USA	4d 15h 37m	5.60
1939	Nordwind	85/25.9	Kreigsmarine	GER	3d 20h 58m	6.51
1963	Gitana	90/27.6	Baron Edmund de Rothschild	FRA	3d 9h 40m	7.41
1971	American Eagle	58/17.7	Ted Turner	USA	3d 7h 11m 48s	7.64
1983	Condor	78/23.8	Bob Bell	GBR	2d 23h 2m 10s	8.50
1985	Nirvana	80/24.4	Martin Green	USA	2d 12h 41m	9.97
1999	RF Yachting	80/24.4	Ross Field	NZL	2d 5h 8m 51s	11.38
1999	Fujicolor II (Multihull)	60/18.3	Loïck Peyron	FRA	1d 16h 27m 0s	14.96

Every other August a large fleet (nowadays about 230 each time) of ocean racers sails the 605-mile Fastnet course. Only gradually has the best average speed increased.

Over the years, the Fastnet race record time very slowly reduced. In 1928 the 55ft (16.8m) US schooner Nina sailed the 605-mile course with the best average of 5.6 knots. This speed was not to be beaten for eleven years.

race to Spain (under a different rule of rating), went from the end of that race to compete in the Fastnet. She made a best average speed round the course of 5.60 knots and also won the event.

By 1939, yachts had been designed and built for ocean racing for some years and the time was reduced to 3d 20h 58m by the Kreigsmarine-owned 85 ft (25.9m) *Nordwind* (Ger), giving 6.51 knots. The yacht was captured by the British in 1945.

In the 26 Fastnet races between 1947 and 1999, there were just seven steps up in best speed, plus one extra when multihulls were eventually permitted to compete (see list). It can be seen that the boats were big and, to those familiar with ocean racing, well known and regular competitors on the major world courses. The owners were also prominent: Ross Field, Ted Turner, Martin Green, Loïck Peyron, Baron Edmund de Rothschild. Such speeds, even if the increments are small, did not come easily.

In this list, *American Eagle* (USA) was an ex-America's Cup 12-metre converted for ocean racing and successful on corrected time as well as elapsed, despite being originally designed for a totally different life. The very handsome *Nirvana* (USA) uniquely held both the Fastnet and the Newport to Bermuda race records simultaneously. I was on this 1985 Fastnet race, when strong to gale winds throughout gave reaches around almost the whole course. As (thank goodness!) such conditions did not repeat themselves for a number of years, this record was unbroken until 1999.

For many years the attractive maxi ocean racer Nirvana held both Fastnet and Bermuda race (and other) records. In her day, big, usually American, monohulls 'ruled'. In later years came challenge from the French ocean multihulls.

Best elapsed time in the first Fastnet race, 1925, 6 days 2 hours 45 minutes (4.26 knot average), was achieved by Jolie Brise, built in 1913 as one of the last sailing pilot cutters.

Multihulls had been allowed in the event from 1997 and thus two records now exist; both achieved in 1999. *RF Yachting* (Nzl), skippered by Ross Field, was an 80ft (24.4m) monohull racer which had competed in a round the world (Whitbread) race; she was timed at 2d 5h 8m 51s (11.38 knots). It had taken 74 years to increase the average best (monohull) speed on the Fastnet race by 7.12 knots: this is an important marker in contemplating the speed of sailing vessels.

The same year the outright record leapt to a new order: the 60ft (18.3m) trimaran *Fujicolor II*, Loïck Peyron (Fra), sailed the 605-mile classic course in 1d 16h 27m 0s (14.96 knots). Thus modern sailing speed reduced the Fastnet from a week's expedition to an overnight race.

6

Around the planet

Arthur Ransome wrote: 'Captain Slocum's place in history is as secure as Adam's.' He was referring, of course, to Joshua Slocum, the first man to sail alone around the world and his account in an 'immortal' book. 'It has inspired and will inspire many other voyages,' said Ransome. 'No other man can be the first.'

Slocum (USA) took three years, from Boston to Boston, calling at many ports on a westabout route, but going through the Strait of Magellan and via the Cape of Good Hope. Speed had nothing to do with it, but the story of times and speeds for yacht circumnavigations of the world had to be built on a foundation of successful cruises and suitable routes.

Joshua Slocum's *Spray* was the first small yacht, as well as the first single-hander. There is a popular association between sailing yachts and circumnavigation. When a yacht is described or shown to people who are ignorant of the sea, they frequently ask 'Could it sail around the world?'

Early roundings

Here is a chronology of circumnavigation. The first ever was by Juan del Elcano and 17 surviving crew in the 85-ton, 120ft (36m) *Vittoria*, which returned to Spain in 1522; all that remained of a three-year five-ship expedition headed by the Portuguese Ferdinand Magellan.

In 1847 HMS *Driver* became the first powered ship to circumnavigate, refuelling at various ports. It is interesting that the British navy had to use sailing ships for distant operations for some years, as their range was not limited by refuelling requirements.

The first private yacht to voyage around was the 170ft (51.8m) three-masted auxiliary schooner *Sunbeam* owned by Lord Brassey (Gbr). His family and guests were attended by a paid crew of thirty. In the years 1876–77, the yacht sailed from Cowes, England, to Magellan Strait (remember the Panama Canal was not yet built) to Japan, the Red Sea, Suez Canal,

The first single-hander to sail around the world without any stop and without assistance was Robin Knox-Johnston (Gbr) in Suhaili in 1968–9.

Mediterranean, England. *Spray*'s voyage, as mentioned, was from 1895 to 1898.

In 1960 the US nuclear submarine *Triton* circumnavigated the world non-stop and was submerged the whole time.

In 1966–67, Francis Chichester circumnavigated, England to England, single-handed in *Gipsy Moth IV* with just one stop at Sydney, Australia: this had never before been attempted.

The first non-stop yacht voyage around the world was in 1968–69 by Robin Knox-Johnston, single-handed in the 32ft (9.8m) bowsprit ketch *Suhaili*. Her average speed came out at 3.39 knots. These and other yacht voyages will be examined below.

Strangely, non-stop voyages under power are almost unheard of (the USS *Triton* is the exception) and today the fastest non-stop voyage around the world by any ship or boat is under sail and not power. The reason for this is that outside possible trials for armed forces, a power vessel would have to refuel or at least carry so much fuel that passengers and freight would be largely excluded. There is no incentive (although see final comment on page 119).

For circumnavigation speed records today, 'stopping' voyages are of marginal interest. Non-stop is the name of the game in races and individual feats. Yachts calling in at ports need to make large route diversions to sail to them; the total time is meaningless because it depends on how many days it has stopped over; the total time at sea added together is a dubious statistic. An exception to this is the voyager who admits to stopping and receiving assistance, but calls in on a 'pit stop', by choice or in emergency, and leaves as soon as possible. Here the clock 'ticks all the time' and thus an assisted circumnavigation is achieved in as fast a time as was possible.

Round the world criteria

Before looking at some past, recent and current circumnavigation records, it is useful to check the present WSSRC definition of a voyage around the planet. What actually constitutes a circumnavigation is not so obvious. A problem arises because if passage times and speeds result for record purposes, then there must be a defined route. The earth is an approximate sphere and to round it one would track along a maximum circumference.

This is possible in theory by an aircraft. Indeed it has been done by special lightweight endurance flying machines and an individual traveller in 2000 made a trip along the equator using various forms of land and sea transport as he went; but not by sea because land is 'in the way'. Sailing from, say, Australia into the Southern Ocean, voyaging around Antarctica and returning to Australia from the 'other' direction, is not a circumnavigation; it would be little different from sailing around 'the rim' of the Pacific Ocean. Both would resemble geometrical segments.

When WSSRC took responsibility for ocean passages, it was unable to find an agreed definition. Admittedly there were general acceptances of round the world voyages, but these do not pose problems until times and

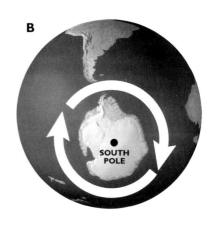

Key

Start 'E' in Europe – – – – – – –

Start 'Z' in New Zealand ··················

C – The five great Capes

'B' Bermuda – rounding for southern
                 hemisphere starter

*The definition of sailing around the world had to be pinned down, once yachts began to claim circumnavigation records. **A** There is no 'natural' circumnavigation on the sea because the land is 'in the way'. **B** Around Antarctic is not 'round the world'. **C** So the distance is made equivalent to that along the equator and the necessities of the route are defined.*

speeds are claimed; the latter were and are the business of the WSSRC.

Francis Chichester and Norris McWhirter (of general records fame) came up with a definition which involved a vessel passing through ante-nodal points. These were points exactly on the circumference pierced by a diameter from the first point (maybe in the English Channel) which arose at the other point (near New Zealand). This was unsatisfactory because it relied on navigating to the point and being satisfied of having passed through it or at least on the longer side of it. In Chichester's day there was no GPS and communication to validate this and even now GPS positions are not accepted as rounding points. Enquiries were made to navigational and geographic institutions, but it turned out that such bodies as the National Geographic (USA) and the Royal Institute of Navigation (Gbr) had not considered the issue.

Various elements were put into a draft definition which was floated past all those interested; it was then tidied up and published. It comprised precedent, practical and existing routes, global distances and limitations. The current text goes like this:

> *A vessel must start and return to the same point, must cross all meridians of longitude and must cross the equator. She may cross some, but not all, meridians more than once (ie two roundings of Antarctica do not count). The orthodromic track of the vessel must be at least 21600 nautical miles. In calculating this distance, it is to be assumed that the vessel will sail around Antarctica in latitude 64 degrees south. A vessel starting in the southern hemisphere has to round an island or other fixed point in the northern hemisphere that will satisfy the minimum distance requirement.*

This definition was to some extent based on the Vendée Globe race (see below) and the slightly longer Jules Verne (also below). The distance given is equivalent to the equator/circumference described above. Crossing an outward track is not enough; the yacht must be timed back by an observer at the point from which she departed.

It is appreciated by navigators, though not always by the public, that the closer the yacht sails to the Antarctic, the shorter is the distance. In practice, the yacht is unlikely to go as far south as 64 degrees because of ice and unwanted prevailing winds, but a latitude has be assumed for distance purposes. The distance is the rhumb line or great circle. What the yacht shows on her log is not used for record purposes, since, as already pointed out, the best performance often coincides with minimizing the logged distance.

The rule does not state that a vessel must sail south of the 'five great capes' (Cape of Good Hope, Leeuwin, Tasmania, Steward Island (NZ), Horn), but she is bound to do so in order to sail this shortest route. Francis Chichester confirmed this as a feat; he was thinking of it in contrast to a semi-tropical voyage, but now it is not necessary to insist upon this.

Under the rule typical valid circumnavigations are:

1 Westbound in the tropics, *stopping*, from Gibraltar–Atlantic–Panama Canal–Pacific–Indian Ocean–Suez Canal–Gibraltar

2 Eastbound from west coast of France or east coast of USA–down the Atlantic–Cape of Good Hope–south of five great capes–the Horn–up the Atlantic–back to starting point

3 The same route but westbound

4 Perth, Australia-south of four capes including the Horn-up the Atlantic–rounding Bermuda–Cape of Good Hope–Perth.

Slowly round

After Joshua Slocum, yacht circumnavigations were few, far between, brave, slow and, of course, stopping. The second man to sail around the world single-handed was another American, Harry Pidgeon, in a 35ft (10.7m) yawl, *Islander*, in 1921–25. By now the Panama Canal was open and his cruising route was Los Angeles–South Sea islands–north of Australia–Cape of Good Hope–Panama–Los Angeles.

It should be remembered that this was the era of total amateurism, with enthusiasm the only spur. There were no communications, except collecting and sending mail in port, and *Islander* was simply a hard chine home-built yacht – the design available for $10 by applying to a yachting magazine. News of such a trip, if any, would be a few lines in a newspaper one day, received as a despatch from a foreign correspondent.

Meanwhile the first yacht circumnavigation via the Southern Ocean was probably the 42ft (12.8m) ketch *Saoirse*, sailed by Conor O'Brien (Irl) and three crew. Her route was Dublin–Cape Town–Melbourne (north of Tasmania)–Cook Strait–Auckland–Cape Horn–Dublin. For running, the yacht was equipped with a squaresail and studding sails. The total time means little, owing to the stops and diversions, but to get an idea of speed, her passage from Auckland round Cape Horn to Port Stanley, Falkland Islands, took 46 days for the 5800 miles, giving an average of 5.25 knots.

The first single-hander to sail round Cape Horn on a voyage and survive was the Argentinian Vito Dumas in the ketch *Lehg II*. In 1942 during WWII, he left Buenos Aires for Cape Town, thence south of Australia–Wellington, New Zealand–Cape Horn–Buenos Aires. Total time was 272 days.

A Norwegian, Al Hansen, in the 36ft (11.0m) *Mary Jane*, had rounded the Horn in 1933, east to west, but immediately afterwards the boat was wrecked and the skipper was lost. The rarity of such voyages is shown by the statistic that between 1945 and 1960 there were just five single-handed circumnavigations.

The perils of the Southern Ocean route were shown in February 1957. The 46ft (14.0m) ketch *Tzu Hang* (Gbr), bound from Melbourne and heading for Cape Horn with an experienced crew of three, was pitchpoled and lost total rig, rudder and all deck structure, leaving a gaping hole. As usual there were no communications; the crew just managed to save the boat, make a jury rig and reach South America after six weeks. Nine months later after repairs, making again for Cape Horn, the yacht was knocked down and dismasted; again the crew made harbour unassisted.

Race around? Never!

In 1966 came the first attempt to 'race' in a yacht around the world and through the Southern Ocean. It was to be done from England to England eastabout with only one stop, which would be Sydney, Australia.

The lone skipper was Francis Chichester (Gbr) in *Gipsy Moth IV*, 54ft (16.5m), specially designed for the project by Illingworth & Primrose, much respected for conventional ocean racers.

Chichester set off from Plymouth on 27 August 1966, with the aim of beating the times of nineteenth century clipper ships on the route. His confidence had its origins in his successes in the 1960 and 1964 east-to-west transatlantic races (OSTAR). Some people said that this was impossible; articles in English and Australian newspapers by authors, ranging from respected seamen of the old sailing ships to a popular clairvoyant, declared that Chichester, who was 65 years of age, would come to grief, probably at

The achievement of Francis Chichester in the specially designed Gipsy Moth IV showed that a single-handed one-stop circumnavigation was possible. One year later, non-stop contenders set off.

the feared Cape Horn, where even great square riggers had foundered.

As we all know, *Gipsy Moth IV* duly made the single stop in Sydney. She spent a total of 226 days at sea and averaged 5.71 knots. Chichester returned to England to astonishing scenes of acclaim and great crowds in Plymouth and London, where he was knighted by the Queen as he came ashore from the yacht at Greenwich.

From this distance, such fame is seen as perfectly valid. He was surely the man who began the 'yacht racing rush' around the world. Before him the majority view of the sailing experts was that yacht racing around the world was just fantasy. After him, it progressed in extent and in passage records, as shown below. His achievement did not go unnoticed by the much younger Eric Tabarly, who had beaten him in the 1964 OSTAR; the French reputation for fast ocean sailing was also in the making.

In 1968, it appeared that several sailors were thinking independently about the next step: this was sailing around the world non-stop. A London newspaper took the opportunity to turn this into a kind of race. A voyager could leave at any time within a prescribed period in 1968, from a port in the northern hemisphere, and return there having made no stops after sailing south of the five great capes. The best time would win and there would be a further prize for the first home. Francis Chichester was an adviser to the scheme.

This was the notorious Golden Globe race. The only boat to finish was the 32ft (9.7m) ketch *Suhaili* sailed by Robin-Knox Johnston (Gbr). He arrived back at his departure port, Falmouth, south-west England, on 22 April 1969, after completing the course in 313 days. The average speed was 3.39 knots. This made him the first person on earth to circumnavigate the world single-handed non-stop. Another Adam.

The notorious Golden Globe

Among the nine original contestants:
Chay Blyth had to give up with technical failures before Cape Town, as did four others.
Donald Crowhurst, in a small multihull, deceived the organizers about his route and then committed suicide by throwing himself off the boat.
Bernard Moitessier in the steel *Joshua* (named after Slocum) circled the world more than once, but then sailed on and stayed in the South Seas instead of returning to France.
Nigel Tetley's small multihull broke up in the Atlantic on the return trip and he later committed suicide.

The world had been circumnavigated: What next? Better speed? Women? Multihulls? Actually the next step was to sail 'the wrong way round'. The year after *Suhaili* returned, Chay Blyth, who had recently rowed across the North Atlantic in a two-man boat, left Hamble, England, single-handed in a 59ft (18m) steel cutter, *British Steel*. He sailed *westabout* south of the five capes and returned to Hamble after 293 days (3.85 knots). He was thus not only first to sail the wrong way, but then held the best time for any non-stop boat, single-handed or crewed.

Regular races

Despite caution after the Golden Globe, the next logical step was a properly organized crewed race. Various people had a hand in this, but the event took shape under the flag of the Royal Naval Sailing Association with some sponsorship by the Whitbread Brewery. It was to be fully crewed, under current ocean racing rules (so the winner would be on corrected time), for a wide range of sizes.

Starting at Portsmouth, England, on 8 September 1973, the race would stop and restart at certain ports. For the first four races (1973, 1977, 1981, 1985) these were almost the same: Cape Town–Auckland (Sydney in 1973) –a south American port (Mar del Plata until the Falklands war, then Punta del Este). The 1973–74 race was completed by 14 yachts and won by a production Swan 65 designed by Sparkman & Stephens; she was the Mexican *Sayula*, 65ft (19.6m), owner Ramon Carlin. The best elapsed time was by the 72ft (21.9m) *Great Britain II* (Gbr), Chay Blyth, which had an aggregate time of 144d 10h; average speed 7.82 knots. Round the world speeds were evidently beginning to pick up, but this was a 'stopper' with considerable maintenance, resting and reprovisioning at ports of call.

Run every 4 years, the event soon became known as the Whitbread (the Royal Navy in due course pulled out completely), as the brewery injected more money and control. Whitbread sold out to Volvo motors before the eighth race, which began in 2001. There is a difficulty with records for this Whitbread/Volvo circumnavigation. After the fourth race, the course was changed radically and in the following events it was changed yet again. It became impossible to break records when there was no previous time to better.

Some times in this event remain notable. As it progressed, the boats became larger; then for 1993 the handicapping was dropped altogether. From 1997, the race was restricted to yachts designed to a formula rule, giving a length of about 64ft (19.5m). In 1985–86, the last run on the 'old' course, the best time was by *UBS Switzerland* (Swi), 80ft (24.3m), skipper Pierre Fehlmann; 117d 14h 31m 42s, a leap to 9.61 knots.

The record for one of the established legs, from Auckland to Punta del Este, 5914 miles, is 21d 2h 26m 13s (11.68 knots). A very long leg on a later course in 1993–94 was the 7875 miles from Punta del Este, eastward to Fremantle, Australia, on which the Whitbread 60 class sloop *Intrum Justitia*, skipper Lawrie Smith (Gbr) with a European crew, took 25d 14h 39m 6s. This average of 13 knots is a huge speed to be attained over such a distance. *It is probably the highest speed averaged by a monohull on a passage over, say, 7500 nautical miles.* As mentioned, the races starting in 1997 and 2001 had so many novel stops and diversions that record times are not applicable.

After the first RNSA/Whitbread race, some people were still thinking in terms of beating sailing ship times, as in a 'one-off' race in 1975 from London to London and stopping only at Sydney. The purpose was to beat the time set on this route by the clipper *Patriarch*, 223ft (68.0m), in 1869. Only four boats competed.

Patriarch had taken 69 days to Sydney and the winning yacht for the first leg, *Great Britain II* (Gbr), did it in 67 days 8 hours; distance 13650 miles and speed 8.45 knots, which beat the clipper by about two and a half days. On the return, via Cape Horn, *GBII* 'beat' *Patriarch* by three days and this resulted in an average for the total voyage of 8.2 knots. These voyages do seem to have been the longest fully crewed yacht racing legs to that date.

About the time of the first Whitbread race, Alain Colas (Fra) set off single-handed in the 67ft (20.4m) trimaran *Manureva* (ex-*Pen Duick IV* owned by Eric Tabarly). The voyage was to St Malo and back, stopping only at Sydney. Total time at sea was 168 days; average speed 7.34 knots.

Before the Whitbread races, the number of yachts which had circum-navigated the world, south of the five capes, could be counted in single figures, and the names listed in a few lines. After these races and others mentioned below, I and many others lost count and any actual number (at a guess about 250) came to mean little.

Events, attempts and their records

Single-handed, stopping

For a change this single-handed circumnavigation originated in the USA. David White of Newport, RI, envisaged a stopping event (still under the influence of Golden Globe) from there. A sponsor was found in BOC and the BOC Challenge Around Alone started from Newport on 28 August

Single-handers and others

After the first two Whitbreads, the momentum was increasing for more extreme exploits in circumnavigation. Each event would have its own and, on occasions, overall speed records. They would either be a conventional race or a race against time by attacking the existing record. The categories could almost be created by sitting down and thinking about them. Organizing them on the water was a different business. Here they are summarized; all are circumnavigations via the Southern Ocean.

- **Single-handed race with stops** Created in the USA, this started in 1982 as the BOC Around Alone race.
- **All-women crew with stops** Started with a boat in the 1989 Whitbread and in later races.
- **Single-handed woman with stops and non-stop**
- **Single-handed organized race with no stops** The Vendée Globe was first run in 1989.
- **Fully organized race crewed with stops, but westabout** Organized by Chay Blyth in special one-design ocean racers from 1989.
- **Fastest vessel around the world individual attempt** Fully crewed multihulls for Jules Verne Trophy; first achieved 1993–94.
- **Two or more complete circumnavigations without stopping** In practice achieved by a single-hander on individual initiative.
- **A fully organized race around the world under sail with no limitations** Run as 'The Race'/ *La Course du Millénaire*, started 31 December 2000.

It is difficult to envisage what is left to achieve! Passage records under sail as a result of these challenges and events will now be examined.

1982 with 17 monohull starters. Stops were to be at Cape Town, Sydney, Rio de Janeiro, then return to Newport, RI.

Ten boats completed the course. *Gipsy Moth V*, sailed by Desmond Hampton and borrowed from the Chichester family, ran aground and was wrecked, and two other competitors sank, but each sailor was rescued by another skipper in the race.

The best aggregate time was by Philippe Jeantot in *Crédit Agricole*, 60ft (18.3m), in 159d 2h 26m. Two years later, the winner was again Jeantot, this time in the same sized *Crédit Agricole III*; time: 134d 5h 23m. The stops were the same; there were 25 starters; 18 finishers; one skipper rescued from his liferaft, one skipper lost and his empty yacht found at sea. The third race (Punta del Este substituted for Rio) in 1990–91 retains the record, despite further races every four years. This was by Christophe Auguin in *Group Sceta* (Fra), 60ft (18.3m), who took 120d 22h 36m 35s (9.30 knots).

Single-handed women with stops and non-stop

In the case of women, it is still possible to list all reported circum-navigations, the numbers being a fraction of the total. Women had, on many occasions, sailed with men in small boats around the world, taking an equal part in all aspects of handling and navigating the vessel. An example is Susan Hiscock, who, always alone but for her husband Eric, circumnavigated in the 30ft (9.1m) cutter *Wanderer III* in 1952–55 and twice subsequently.

The first woman to set off on a successful single-handed voyage around the world is believed to be Krystyna Chojnowska-Liskiewicz (Poland) in the 31ft (9.4m) *Mazurek*, from Las Palmas and return via the tropical route and Panama Canal. Meanwhile in 1977, Brigitte Oudry (Fra) sailed single-handed around south of Cape of Good Hope, Leeuwin and Horn in *Gea*, 34ft (10.4m), also stopping. In the same year, in the sponsored 53ft (16.1m)

Single-handed women sailing around the world

ACHIEVEMENT	DATE	NAME	NAT	YACHT	LOA ft/m
First ever, Las Palmas via Panama Canal	1976-78	Krystyna Chojnowska-Liskiewicz	POL	*Mazurek*	31/9.4
First south of three capes, stopping	1977	Brigitte Oudry	FRA	*Gea*	34/10.4
First south of all great capes, stopping from/to Dartmouth	1977	Dame Naomi James	GBR/NZL	*Express Crusader*	53/16.1
First non-stop from/to Sydney, 189d	1988	Kay Cottee (now Sutton)	AUS	*Blackmore's First Lady*	37/11.3
From/to Kagoshima, Japan, South of Three capes (Notnz), 278d	1992	Kyoko Imakiire	JAP	*Kairen*	35/10.7
Non-stop, timed by WSSRC, to/from Dartmouth	1995	Lisa Clayton (now Viscountess Cobham)	GBR	*Spirit of Birmingham*	38/11.6
Westabout, stopping, to/from Plymouth	1996	Samantha Brewster	GBR	*Heath Insured II*	67/20.4
Non-stop fastest to date, 140d	1997	Catherine Chabaud	FRA	*Whirlpool-Europe 2*	60/18.3
Current non-stop fastest, 94d	2001	Ellen MacArthur	GBR	*Kingfisher*	60/18.3

cutter *Express Crusader*, Naomi James sailed from England to make the first female non-stop circumnavigation. However she was forced to put in at Cape Town and then again at Port Stanley, Falkland Islands, to seek assistance in making repairs. She did complete the voyage, including stops, in 272 days which is a (theoretical) average of 3.33 knots.

The first woman to make a single-handed non-stop voyage around the world was an Australian from Sydney to Sydney eastabout and taking in the St Peter and Paul rocks off Brazil in the northern hemisphere. This was Kay Cottee in the 37ft (11.3m) sloop *Blackmore's First Lady*. She returned to Sydney on 5 June 1988, after 189 days, at an average of 5.51 knots.

In 1991–92 the Japanese woman Kyoko Imakiire in *Kairen*, 35ft (10.7m), sailed single-handed from Kagoshima eastabout via Cape Horn–Cape of Good Hope–Tasmania and back to the start point in 278 days. She did not round New Zealand.

None of the above fitted the WSSRC criteria for circumnavigation speeds, because they did not exist at the time, but Kay Cottee (now Sutton) rounded the rocks north of the equator in the Atlantic in accordance with the recommendations of Nobby Clarke. She has to be regarded as the first ever female non-stop single-hander.

In 1994–95 Lisa Clayton (Gbr) sailed single-handed from Dartmouth, England and back to Dartmouth south of all five great capes in accordance with, and timed by, WSSRC rules. In the 38ft (11.6m) sloop *Spirit of Birmingham* she took 285 days; average 3.18 knots. After she finished there was a highly publicized controversy, because she had anchored in the harbour at Cape Town. She claimed to have received no contact or assistance, though people remained afloat close to the boat. There was also an unfortunate lack of evidence about her track, compounded by the secretiveness of her shore manager. However, after much inaccurate press comment, the voyage was duly ratified. But in record terms the slow speed prevented this passage being any sort of landmark.

Notable speed only came when women crews were alone on racers. The Whitbread of 1989–90 saw the first all-women crew in this stopping event. Tracy Edwards (Gbr) and an international crew of 11 completed the course in the sloop *Maiden*, 58ft (17.7m), in an aggregate 167d 3h 6m 53s. All-women crews sailed on subsequent occasions in this event.

For single-handed, non-stop achievement by women, the arena duly became the Vendée Globe (see below). On two occasions the established long-distance sailor Isabelle Autissier (Fra) had to give up after dismasting or capsize, but in 1996–96 Catherine Chabaud (Fra) in the Open 60 class, 60ft (18.3m) *Whirlpool-Europe 2* completed the non-stop course in 140d 4h 38m 45s (6.46 knots).

Kingfisher *was specially designed for the 2000–1 non-stop single-handed race around the world. Ellen MacArthur achieved records of fastest woman and second fastest single-hander in 94 days 4 hours 25 minutes.*

About the same time, Samantha Brewster (Gbr) was the first woman to sail westabout south of all the great capes, though forced to stop for repairs once. Sailing the 67ft (20.4m) *Heath Insured II*, one of the relatively heavy steel one-designs intended for a large crew belonging to Chay Blyth, was 247d 14h 51m 7s (3.66 knots). However, this remains the record for this category.

In 1998, in the 92ft (28.0m) catamaran *Royal & Sun Alliance*, Tracy Edwards and her all-woman crew attempted a circumnavigation from Brest, but the vessel was dismasted in the Southern Ocean and ended the voyage in a port in Chile.

Then in the year 2001, in the Vendée Globe, Ellen MacArthur, single-handed in the specially designed and built Open 60 *Kingfisher*, 60ft (18.3m), smashed all previous female times and the previous (male) monohull single-handed time. Indeed, at second in the race, she narrowly missed the outright single-handed circumnavigation record. She finished at Les Sables d'Olonne in 94d 4h 25m 40s. This gave an average of 9.63 knots; as previously pointed out on more than one occasion, that means that the speed was considerably more (twice or more) at times.

Single-handed race with no stops

After Philippe Jeantot won the first two BOC Around Alone races, he decided to organize a non-stop version of the event from France.

Meanwhile, it must be mentioned that there had been two individual non-stop circumnavigations which had improved the 1971 time of Chay Blyth. John Ridgway (Gbr) (who had rowed across the Atlantic with Blyth) and Andy Briggs made a non-stop two-man circumnavigation from Scotland and back in *English Rose V*, 48ft (14.6m), in 193 days (6.48 knots); then Dodge Morgan (USA) went around, leaving Bermuda in November 1985 and returning there, non-stop and alone in *American Promise* in 150 days (7.07 knots). This yacht began to foreshadow the modern era in that she carried all available electronic and communication aids; previously this had been mimimal.

To return to the visionary Philippe Jeantot and his plans which in time were to become so important. The rules of his race were to be simple (I was on the jury): one person on board, monohulls (no multis), overall length maximum 60ft, no outriggers, and that was all. Eventually, later versions of

Round the world non-stop: progressive records

YEAR	SKIPPER	YACHT	NAT	START/FINISH	DAYS	SPEED	CREW
1968-69	Robin Knox-Johnston	*Suhaili*	GBR	Falmouth, England	313	3.39	Single-handed
1970-71	Chay Blyth	*British Steel*	GBR	Solent, England	293	3.85	Single-handed
1983-84	John Ridgway	*English Rose V*	GBR	Scotland	193	6.48	2-handed
1985-86	Dodge Morgan	*American Promise*	USA	Bermuda	150	7.07	Single-handed
1989-90	Titouan Lamazou	*Ecureuil d'Aquitaine*	FRA	Sables d'Olonne, Fr	109	8.23	Single-handed
1993-94	Bruno Peyron	*Commodore Explorer*	FRA	Brest, France	79	11.35	Crew
1994-95	Robin Knox-Johnston/ Peter Blake	*Enza*	GBR/ NZL	Brest, France	74	12.00	Crew
1997	Olivier de Kersauson	*Sport Elec*	FRA	Brest, France	71	12.66	Crew

Increase of circumnavigation speeds.

Single-handed progressive after 1990

YEAR	SKIPPER	YACHT	NAT	START/FINISH	DAYS	SPEED
1997	Christophe Auguin	*Geodis*	FRA	Sables d'Olonne	105	9.56
2001	Michel Desjoyeaux	*PRB*	FRA	Sables d'Olonne	93	9.73

Single-handed, but no longer outright speeds.

the event had some additional rules, mainly involving stability and other security aspects. The race was – and always has been since – started and finished from the yachting, fishing and holiday port of Le Sables d'Olonne on the Atlantic coast north of La Rochelle. The department (region) called Vendée supported the event, which was also kindly given a part English name: Vendée Globe.

Enthusiasm was immediate and the resort opened up in a normally closed season: November 1989. Thirteen boats started and seven of those finished correctly. The elapsed time was a leap for single-handed circum-navigations: 109d 8h 48m 50s (8.23 knots) by *Ecureuil d'Aquitaine* (Fra), 60ft (18.3m), sailed by Titouan Lamazou. On his return to France he had a hero's welcome both at the finish and later in the centre of Paris. He was decorated by the President of the Republic.

This time of 109 days had an electrifying effect on the leading edge of sailing. It meant that ten boats were specifically designed and built for the next Vendée and others began to think about how it could be reduced in other craft.

In the record of non-stop single-handers, before 1990 only four people had ever achieved this: Robin Knox-Johnston (Gbr), Chay Blyth (Gbr), Kay Cottee (Aus) and Dodge Morgan (USA). After 1990, these four were joined by seven Frenchmen.

In the second Vendée Globe in 1992, 14 sailors started. The winner, Alain Gautier (Fra) in *Bagages Supérior*, took 110d 10m so the record was not broken, though the time/speed was amazingly consistent. Only eight finished. One sailor was lost at sea; others sought refuge at various stages.

In 1996–97, in a Vendée notable for capsizes, rescues, damage and another death, the record was broken by a few days. *Geodis*, as ever an Open 60, sailed alone by Christophe Auguin, finished in 105d 20h 31m 23s, giving 9.56 knots. Then at the finish in February 2001, this was eclipsed not only by Ellen MacArthur, mentioned above, who was second, but by the winner and new record holder for single-handed circumnavigation in any vessel, Michel Desjoyeaux (Fra) in *PRB*, who took an outstanding 93d 3h 57m 32s (9.73 knots).

Opposite: In February 1990 Ecureuil d'Aquitaine, sailed alone by Titouan Lamazou, circumnavigated the world in 109 days 8 hours 48 minutes 50 seconds. This was the best time of any sailing vessel and he was acclaimed a hero in France.

Fully organized race, crewed with stops, westabout

Chay Blyth, as recounted, had sailed around the world 'against the weather' in *British Steel* many years previously. In 1992 he organized a race on such a course for one-design 67ft (20.4m) offshore yachts, designed by David Thomas (Gbr). These were built, all alike, of steel in England and manned by amateur but duly trained crews with professional skippers and back-up.

The race was a stopper, starting and finishing near Southampton, England, and calling at Rio, rounding Cape Horn, Auckland, Sydney, Cape Town and back to the start. Later races varied the course slightly with ports in the USA, but always it was westabout around Cape Horn. This is very interesting because of the tendency of traditional sailing ships to be unable to weather the Horn. None of Blyth's vessels has ever run back from the Horn, though there have inevitably been ups and downs elsewhere. The course does not lend itself to records, but is mentioned as an important part of yacht circumnavigation. The races were in 1992–93, 1996–97 and 2000–1; for the latter, a new twelve-strong fleet of 75ft (22.9m) yachts had been built mostly in England (but two in China) to a design by Rob Humphreys.

Single-handed westabout non-stop race

The voyage of Samantha Brewster, who was forced to stop for repairs, is mentioned above under *women*. Using another Blyth vessel, 67ft (20.4m), Mike Golding (Gbr) sailed from England and back, westward around the Horn and south of all capes in 161d 16h 32m 24s (5.61 knots) breaking Chay Blyth's long-held record. This was in turn broken by Philippe Monnet in *Uunet*, 60ft (18.3m), whom we have met before, from Brest, France, and back on the same route taking 151d 19h 54m 36s (5.97 knots). This remains the record for single-handers in any vessel on this demanding course.

Unusual circumnavigations

Fastest vessel of any kind around the world – individual attempt

Titouan Lamazou's record of 109 days was created to be beaten, but not immediately, by another single-handed Open 60. From the fictional book by Jules Verne, *Round the World in Eighty Days*, came the title of a new trophy: the Jules Verne Trophy which would be awarded to whoever could sail around the world inside 80 days. The start and finish had to be on a line joining Ushant, the exposed island at the west of Brittany, and Lizard Point, the most southern point of England which is also near its furthest west. In practice, the boats have invariably started near Ushant, as it makes the voyage shorter.

The attempts have been in multihulls of 75ft (22.9m) upwards, fully crewed. There have been occasional false starts and returns (and see the account of Tracy Edwards and crew given above), but as the attempt is individual, the boat can start again to her own programme.

The 80-day challenge was broken, just, by Bruno Peyron (Fra) in the 85ft (25.9m) catamaran *Commodore Explorer* in 1993–94. The passage was 79 days (11.35 knots). The next year Robin Knox-Johnston (Gbr) and Peter Blake (Nzl) and crew in the catamaran *Enza*, 92ft (28.0m), broke this firmly by 5 days with a speed of 12.00 knots. In 1997 came another French challenge by Olivier de Kersauson and crew in the trimaran *Sport Elec*, 90ft (27.4m). He still (2002) holds the outright sailing circumnavigation of the world and the Jules Verne Trophy in a time of 71d 14h 22m 8s, an average of 12.66 knots.

Two or more complete single-handed circumnavigations without stopping

This amazing feat remains the achievement of Jon Sanders of Perth, Australia. In 1981 he sailed the S&S 34 design *Perie Banou* from

Round the world in 80 days was the challenge and this was first achieved in 79 days by Bruno Peyron in Commodore Explorer *in 1993–94.*

A succession of fully crewed circumnavigations in the 1990s reduced the time taken. Enza was the Anglo-New Zealand success the following year, taking only 74 days. Two years later, she was beaten by yet another French crew with a three-day reduction.

Fremantle, Western Australia, south of New Zealand, past Cape Horn north to Plymouth, England, where he sailed around the breakwater but did not stop; then south of all the capes including Cape Horn again and through the Southern Ocean to Fremantle. Thus sailing twice around; but that was not enough for Sanders.

During 1986–88, in the specially re-rigged and strengthened sloop *Parry Endeavour*, 44ft (13.4m), he made a triple circumnavigation: three times through the Southern Ocean. His route from Fremantle started west against the prevailing wind: Cape of Good Hope, up the Atlantic around St Peter and Paul rocks, Cape Horn westward, round a buoy off Fremantle without stopping, then eastabout, the Horn, Peter and Paul, Cape of Good Hope, Fremantle buoy again, on eastward, the Horn, Peter and Paul, Cape of Good Hope, Fremantle. The total was about 71000 miles; the time was 657 days at sea. Will it ever be repeated?

Fully organized race around the world under sail with no limitations

Bruno Peyron, who had been the first skipper to win the Jules Verne, planned this race for a celebration of the new millennium. He obtained major sponsorship from the French government millennium commission, Disneyland Paris and Renault cars. It was to be called simply 'The Race' or '*La Course du Millénaire*'. The starting date was to be 1 January 2000, but that was postponed to 31 December 2000. Rather oddly the starting place was located inside the Mediterranean at Barcelona and the finish was to be at Marseille further along the coast.

Major new design projects were started; building and trials began and all were up against time. All were multihulls of between 110ft (33.5m) and 135ft (41.1m).

Experienced skippers included Steve Fossett (USA), Cam Lewis (USA), Pete Goss (Gbr), Loïck Peyron (Fra), with Skip Novak (USA), Grant Dalton (Nzl) and Tony Bullimore (Gbr). There were thrills and spills in the trials of all the boats, and Pete Goss and his crew were all rescued when their multihull of radical design sank in the northern North Atlantic in winter weather.

The race mustered six boats which duly started; its course requiring passage through Cook Strait beween the islands of New Zealand. This made it longer in practice than the Jules Verne, but shorter under the rule of the WSSRC, so it could not challenge the world record. The best time of 62d 6h 56m 33s was by the 110ft (33.5m) catamaran *ClubMed*, skippered by Grant Dalton (Nzl), plus an international crew of twelve, on the course as set of 23300 nautical miles with an average speed of 15.58 knots. Sometimes this vessel was sailing at a steady 30 knots, perhaps even faster for periods. Truly, speed under sail on the ocean had succumbed to sailing yacht progress by the year 2001.

7

Day's run

We have seen how some of the more commercially sensitive masters of fast sailing ships, and clippers of the nineteenth century, claimed mileages for an outstanding day's run. There was little difference between the two credible best claims for these distances in 24 hours. *Champion of the Seas*, remember, recorded 467 nautical miles on 11/12 December 1854; *Lightning* posted 430 miles on 11/12 March 1857. The figure of 467 miles gives an average of 19.46 knots. No sailing yacht nor any sailing vessel came anywhere near this for a further 100 years.

Distance run in exactly 24 hours has a peculiar fascination and, indeed, it has valid significance. Before the use of electronics, the only way to fix the position in the open ocean was by an astronomical sight. Noon was the

24-hour distance run: progressive records

YEAR	YACHT	TYPE	LOA ft/m	SKIPPER	NAT	DISTANCE	AV. SPEED
1854	*Champion of the Seas*	Clipper	225/68	–	USA	467	19.46
1984	*Formule Tag*	TRI	75/23	Mike Birch	CAN/GBR	512.5	21.35
1987	*Fleury Michon VIII*	TRI	75/23	Philippe Poupon	FRA	517.0	21.54
1990	*Jet Services V*	CAT	75/22.80	Serge Madec	FRA	522.73	21.85
1994	*Lyonnaise des Eaux*	CAT	75/22.80	Olivier de Kersauson	FRA	524.63	21.91
1994	*Primagaz**	TRI	60/18	Laurent Bourgnon	FRA	540.0	22.50
1994	*Explorer*	CAT	86/26.21	Bruno Peyron	FRA	547.3	22.86
1999	*PlayStation*	CAT	105/32	Steve Fossett	USA	580.23	24.18
2000	*ClubMed*	CAT	110/33.50	Grant Dalton	NZL/FRA	625.7	26.07
2001	*ClubMed*	CAT	110/33	Grant Dalton	NZL/FRA	655.2	27.30
2001	*PlayStation*	CAT	125/38.1	Steve Fossett	USA	687.17	28.63

* Primagaz still (2001) holds single-handed record for this

The original sailing ships made their claims for 24-hour records. These have long since been broken by multihulls and monohulls and further confirmed by modern technology of position finding and communication.

traditional time to take this and was more accurate than at other times of day or night for technical reasons. Thus noon to noon distance was published each day on a voyage; on passenger liners (sail or steam) there was often a sweepstake to guess the figure.

It is also a very useful time period for measuring sustained speed. After all, some prevailing weather can last consistently for about 24 hours, though for longer periods change is likely to lower the speed. Shorter favourable periods might be regarded as freak. Anyway, whatever the reasons, this 24-hour measurement is retained by those who sail the seas and those who own the ships. It is perhaps also a suitable span of speed on which to hang our old friend, the speed/length ratio (speed in knots divided by the square root of length/load waterline in feet). In the case of this record of *Champion of the Seas*, it is 1.28.

Claims and science

The arrival of large multihulls created the possibility of high sustained speeds. These were most likely in transocean races. The first reported claim came in 1984 by the skipper of a 75ft (22.9m) multihull *Formule Tag*, Mike Birch (Can/Gbr), who, during a transatlantic west-to-east race, reported a 24-hour run of 512.5 miles, giving an average of 21.35 knots. This soundly beat the clippers.

On 16/17 June 1987 during the Quebec to St Malo race, when in mid-Atlantic, a trimaran of the same length recorded 517.0 miles in a day. This was Philippe Poupon (Fra) in *Fleury Michon VIII* with an average of 21.54 knots; speed/length ratio: 2.62. Poupon explained that he was, therefore, sailing or surfing at 25 to 30 knots at times during the period.

The problem with these sets of figures was that at such speed the difference between *Formule Tag* and *Fleury Michon VIII* was only 13 minutes of sailing and less than 5 miles, or less than 0.01 per cent. For credibility, some rather accurate positioning and timing devices would appear to have been necessary and meanwhile it was not known on what these early claims were based. Race organizers, the WSSRC and keen sailors looked into the problem closely around 1994–95. They were able to come up with a scheme which had become possible owing to the advance of electronic communication and navigation equipment for yachts.

First, it was necessary to decide what clock times would be used for the record. The old noon-to-noon period was now inappropriate since sextant observations were no longer used. Any time of day or night was available electronically for the start, with another time exactly 24 hours later. Then there must be an independent check which did not rely on the observations and logged figures from the crew. Racing yachts on the ocean had, for some years, been tracked by an Argos transmitter, which the competitor on board was unable to touch (except possibly in an emergency), but which the shore organizers could read.

In 1994 the Argos company, which had its processing offices in Toulouse, France, added a GPS receiver-processor to its transmitter, so that very accurate positions could be read on shore. A third party on shore, equipped with a PC, could access the readings on line. Other companies had developed similar link-ups with SatCom (Satellite Communication). All that now remained was to ensure there was a sealed unit, which the crew could not touch, but which gave positions on shore every few minutes or as demanded.

Since about 1994, the instrumentation has been increasingly refined so that a print-out of the position is displayed on shore, but the crew on board will, of course, also know the GPS positions and the GPS speed and log (in other words, over the sea bottom). The crew can then claim a record against the data which is written down independent of them. The times must be in UTC/GMT to avoid any confusion (it is used within all GPS systems). The time must be exactly 24 hours or less. *If it is more, no extrapolation is allowed; so it is invalid.*

The current WSSRC rule (or rather part of it) thus reads as follows:

> *Timed position reports from the vessel must be GPS positions which are then transmitted onwards to an approved base station or directly to an official observer appointed by WSSRC. The onward transmission may be via Inmarsat, Argos or another system capable of either collecting the data and automatically forwarding it at pre-set intervals, or of being polled by the base station (or both). The essential feature is that the timed GPS position reports must be collected and forwarded without any action by the crew of the vessel.*

If the yacht is part of a race, then arrangements are best made with the race organizers before the start; the latter presumably briefing all skippers upon what exactly is required. If there is an individual attempt, the yacht will be in touch with an approved base, maybe the shore manager's office.

This is an area in sailing speed records which is prone to misunderstanding and failure. It is slightly complex and depends on lines of communication both electronic and human (setting up, maintenance, validity, actual claiming amongst others). Claims almost always occur on a long ocean passage, although in 1999 Steve Fossett and crew in the newly built catamaran *PlayStation* (then 105ft (32.0m) later lengthened) made a 24-hour record during offshore trials off New Zealand, where she had been built.

To go offshore and hang about to find 24 hours of suitable weather is usually a long shot and unattractive. In practice, circumstances occur on a long passage on a day that no one could predict, the speed gathering for record breaking potential. The GPS and Satcom are running, the print gives verification on shore.

Even then the story is not always over, because the WSSRC must be informed in order to ratify the new distance. The world (in the form of the media) tends to get the news first and apparent records have been trumpeted which have failed, because the data are improper or, quite often, no claim is actually made. Was the distance sailed? Who knows? Maybe the figure was not quite right on re-examination; maybe the time on inspection was a few minutes more than 24 hours. For the best 24-hour record, as it exists on any given date, a reference to WSSRC is essential.

Men, multis, monos

As with other passage records there are the following categories:

- Outright (probably, but not necessarily, crewed multihull)
- Crewed mono
- Single-handed – any vessel
- Single-handed mono (if the latter was multi)
- All-women or woman in these four categories.

In practice at this time of writing, not all these categories have ever occurred nor been claimed for a 24-hour distance run.

The first claimant following the establishment of the electronic system was the formula-designed Whitbread 60 Class *Intrum Justitia*, 64ft (19.5m), on a leg in the Southern Ocean of the Whitbread Round the World Race. The skipper was Lawrie Smith (Gbr) with a 'European/Netherlands' crew. The ratified distance in 24 hours was 428 nautical miles. This gave a speed of 17.83 knots and a speed/length ratio of 2.31. If *Fleury Michon VIII*'s record was accepted, then this one was for best monohull. Swiftly after this came a single-handed run by Laurent Bourgnon (Fra) in the 60ft (18.3m) trimaran *Primagaz*. He was single-handed and returning west to east across the Atlantic from New York after the 1994 '*transat anglais*' (OSTAR), the Royal Western Yacht Club's regular Plymouth to Newport, RI, single-handed event. On 28/29 June 1994 he covered 540.0 nautical miles in 24 hours.

This was exactly recorded and ratified; he therefore came to hold the outright record for any yacht and also the single-handed record for any yacht. The average was an amazing 22.50 knots, the speed/length ratio had arrived at a new level of 2.92.

In 1997, the 24-hour monohull record was improved during a leg in the Southern Ocean of the Whitbread Round the World Race for crewed yachts. It was by the same skipper, Lawrie Smith, and same class of yacht, a Whitbread 60 class *Silk Cut*, 64ft (19.5m) (Gbr), which covered 449.1 miles in 24 hours on 19/20 November. This gave 18.71 knots and speed/length ratio of 2.43.

By mid-1998, these two boats, *Primagaz* and *Silk Cut*, were the only holders of 24-hour records, other categories being then unclaimed. It is interesting to note that the ratified distance of *Primagaz* well exceeded the less well attested mileage of *Fleury Michon VIII*; so the latter's record can be said to have been valid, but was then duly beaten.

It took the advent of the 'giant multihulls' preparing for The Race to break the outstanding record of *Primagaz*. On 26/27 March 1999, while on trials and tune-up based in New Zealand (sailing between Norfolk Island and the Great Barrier Reef), Steve Fossett (USA) and his international crew in the 105ft (32.0m) catamaran *PlayStation* recorded 580.23 miles in 24 hours. The average speed was 24.18 knots and the speed/length ratio 2.42. Note

PlayStation, *owned and skippered by Steve Fossett, was one of the monster multi-hulls designed and built for 'The Race', a millennium long distance event. She is holder of the 24-hour longest distance run of any sailing vessel: 687 nautical miles (28.63 knots).*

that the latter was less than *Primagaz* simply because *PlayStation* was so much longer; in other words, she had more potential. *Primagaz* and Laurent Bourgnon retained their single-handed record.

Steve Fossett's historic achievement (longest day's run of any sailing vessel ever) was fairly soon beaten by another giant catamaran. During an individual record attempt of an ocean passage from Cadiz, Spain, to San Salvador in mainly trade wind conditions on 10/11 June 2000, *ClubMed*, 110ft (33.5m), with Grant Dalton (Nzl), Bruno Peyron (Fra) and crew, soundly recorded 625.7 miles. Their speed was 26.1 knots with a speed/length ratio of 2.56. The same boat, skippered by Grant Dalton, smashed her own record during The Race, when in the Southern Ocean about 1300 miles west of Cape Horn. On 8/9 February 2001 she clocked 655.2 miles in 24 hours; average speed an outstanding 27.29 knots. Even this was

nom	Dist 24H	Vit 24H	Cap	Date 1	.	Latitude 1	Longitude 1
Club Med	655.1345	27.30	100	08/02/01 11:00:0		57 53.64' S	108 47.40' W
Club Med	654.939	27.29	101	08/02/01 09:58:0		57 54.92' S	109 38.12' W
Club Med	653.03	27.21	99	08/02/01 12:00:0		57 52.98' S	107 58.02' W
Club Med	652.4261	27.18	101	08/02/01 08:00:0		57 52.92' S	111 23.04' W
Club Med	643.6208	26.82	102	08/02/01 06:00:0		57 49.04' S	113 06.68' W
Club Med	643.3765	26.81	102	08/02/01 07:01:0		57 51.96' S	112 15.78' W
Club Med	642.3682	26.77	102	08/02/01 05:30:0		57 48.20' S	113 31.28' W
Club Med	641.8065	26.74	102	08/02/01 05:00:0		57 47.16' S	113 56.16' W
Club Med	641.5522	26.73	102	08/02/01 05:01:0		57 47.16' S	113 55.80' W
Club Med	640.4025	26.68	102	08/02/01 04:30:0		57 45.60' S	114 20.76' W
Club Med	638.6694	26.61	103	08/02/01 03:30:0		57 45.52' S	115 08.16' W
Club Med	638.4792	26.60	103	08/02/01 03:00:0		57 45.96' S	115 30.48' W
Club Med	638.4735	26.60	102	08/02/01 04:00:0		57 44.28' S	114 46.28' W
Club Med	637.7896	26.57	97	08/02/01 19:30:0		57 49.24' S	101 39.28' W
Club Med	637.2607	26.55	104	08/02/01 02:30:0		57 48.08' S	115 53.88' W
Club Med	636.2606	26.51	97	08/02/01 20:00:0		57 49.20' S	101 15.24' W
Club Med	634.7839	26.45	104	08/02/01 02:00:0		57 50.24' S	116 16.76' W
Club Med	634.4811	26.44	96	08/02/01 20:30:0		57 49.16' S	100 50.84' W
Club Med	634.3315	26.43	97	09/02/01 04:00:0		57 28.84' S	94 58.28' W
Club Med	633.4476	26.39	104	08/02/01 01:30:0		57 52.16' S	116 40.72' W
Club Med	632.9592	26.37	97	09/02/01 04:30:0		57 27.64' S	94 35.44' W
Club Med	632.8675	26.37	97	09/02/01 03:30:0		57 30.84' S	95 22.00' W
Club Med	632.7968	26.37	97	08/02/01 21:30:0		57 47.52' S	100 03.16' W
Club Med	632.3323	26.35	97	09/02/01 05:00:0		57 26.44' S	94 12.08' W
Club Med	631.7133	26.32	97	09/02/01 03:00:0		57 32.48' S	95 45.88' W
Club Med	631.7037	26.32	97	08/02/01 22:00:0		57 46.96' S	99 38.76' W
Club Med	631.6533	26.32	105	08/02/01 01:00:0		57 54.56' S	117 05.48' W
Club Med	631.0272	26.29	96	09/02/01 05.30.0		57 24.92' S	93 49.96' W
Club Med	631.0203	26.29	97	08/02/01 23:04:0		57 44.60' S	98 50.24' W
Club Med	630.8359	26.28	97	09/02/01 02:30:0		57 33.88' S	96 10.00' W
Club Med	630.7079	26.28	97	09/02/01		57 41.84' S	98 07.16' W
Club Med	630.6464	26.28	97	08/02/01 22:30:0		57 45.80' S	99 16.80' W
Club Med	630.2246	26.26	97	08/02/01 23:30:0		57 43.44' S	98 30.68' W
Club Med	630.0959	26.25	96	09/02/01 06:06:0		57 23.16' S	93 22.60' W
Club Med	629.9753	26.25	97	09/02/01 02:00:0		57 35.16' S	96 33.60' W

This print-out shows the plots from ClubMed during her 24-hour record distance run. On such attempts, these figures are recorded at an agreed shore station.

broken on 6/7 October 2001 in the North Atlantic. *PlayStation*, on a west-to-east transatlantic attempt, sailed 687.17 miles in 24 hours (28.63 knots).

The 2000–1 Vendée Globe race for single-handed monohulls produced the first claims for this category in 24-hour runs. In the Southern Ocean on 8/9 December 2000 Dominique Wavre (Fra), racing in *Union Bancaire Privée* 60ft (18.3m), covered 430.7 miles in 24 hours. He achieved a speed of 17.94 knots and speed/length ratio of 2.32. About six weeks later, a boat which had actually retired from the race then undertook a mid-winter west-to-east Atlantic crossing, but this time with a crew of five. She was the Open 60 *Armor Lux*, with skipper Bernard Stamm (Sui), who on 31 January/1 February 2001 sailed 467.7 miles in 24 hours. The average speed was 19.54 knots with a speed/length of 2.54.

Thus by, say, early 2001 the main distinct categories for a day's run had all been fairly recently and most remarkably recorded. There were vacancies in all the women crew categories because no claims had been made, though both female full crews and single-handers had surely made some impressive but unrecorded runs.

8

Sailing firsts and other records

'Firsts' may or may not be records. The first achievement on a declared route (a simple example is the Fastnet race) is recorded until beaten; some firsts are not the sort one 'beats' anyway (first sailing boat with no inside ballast); almost all remain as firsts, however many records follow, as that label cannot be taken away from them. 'Firsts' are a dangerous area for writers, as too often someone pops up and names an earlier happening in the category; but that applies to all 'superlatives', a helpful word given usage by Norris McWhirter, for largest, smallest, oldest, not to mention fastest. This chapter recounts some sailing superlatives, in general leaving aside the speed records which fill most of the rest of this book.

First across oceans

Some world circumnavigation firsts have already been listed. These included:

- First single-handed, Joshua Slocum in *Spray*
- First with only one stop, Francis Chichester in *Gipsy Moth IV*
- First non-stop, Robin Knox-Johnston in *Suhaili*
- First single-handed woman, Krystyna Chojnowska-Liskiewicz in *Mazurek*
- First non-stop single-handed woman, Kay Cottee (now Sutton) in *First Lady*
- First treble circumnavigation, Jon Sanders in *Parry Endeavour*
- First non-stop single-handed westabout, Chay Blyth in *British Steel*
- First woman single-handed westabout south of the capes, Samantha Brewster in *Heath Insured II*.

In this section can be added the youngest single-handed non-stop, Jesse

Martin (Aus), then aged 18, in *Lionheart*, 34ft (10.4m), in 1998; Melbourne, Australia, to Melbourne south of the capes and rounding Bermuda, taking 367 days. A previous claim was by the Japanese Kojiro Shiraishi, who arrived back in Matsuzaki harbour in June 1994, at the age of 26, after 150 days on the Open 50 *Spirit of Yukoh*.

Before them, a stopping (tropical) circumnavigation had been made by Robin Lee Graham (USA), who set out from San Pedro, California in July 1965, aged 16. His boat was 24ft (7.3m), but he changed to another larger one en route. Readers may or may not think this invalidates whatever the claim may be.

Another Australian youth, David Griffith Dicks, born October 1978, in *Seaflight*, 34ft (10.4m), in 1996, sailed Fremantle, Australia, to Fremantle south of all capes and rounding Bermuda.

Many notable ocean voyages were across the Atlantic Ocean. The first known deliberate solo sailing was well before Slocum and was by Alfred Johnson (USA) in the little *Centennial*, 20ft (6.1m), to celebrate the notable date 1876. He took 46 days from Maine to Wales. Two sailors are close as the oldest transatlantic single-hander. One is Mary Harper (USA), aged 79 of Pennsylvania, in *Kuan Yin II*, 30ft (9.1m). In July 1994, she sailed from Long Pond, Newfoundland, to Crosshaven, south-west Ireland (a usefully 'short route across') in 25 days, experiencing a high proportion of head winds. The single-hander Mike Richey (Gbr) in his Folkboat class *Jester II*, 25ft (7.7m), left Newport, RI on 25 June 1997 and arrived without incident at Plymouth, England on 31 July, taking 36 days, during which he celebrated his 80th birthday on 6 July.

A previous holder was Stefan Szwarnowski (Gbr) in *Tawny Pipit*. At the age of 77 (born 1912), he took 72 days from New Jersey to Bude, England in 1989.

In 2000 Helen Tew (Gbr), aged 88, crossed the Atlantic on the Trade wind route from England to English Harbour, Antigua in the Caribbean, crewing with one of her sons (in his 60s) on the 26ft (7.9m) gaff cutter, *Mary Helen*; she kept watch four hours on and off. In 2001, now of course 89, Mrs Tew sailed back to England in the same boat. She had previously made many voyages including one to the Faeroe Islands from south-west England in 'a seven tonner' (as was the terminology then) of which she wrote an account in 1929.

In 1934 her father, Commander Douglas Graham RN, made a northern westward voyage across the Atlantic in a 30ft (9.1m) cutter from Falmouth, England, to St John's, Newfoundland. At the time this was considered extremely daring. The Royal Cruising Club had to make excuses for awarding him its prize, saying that while it did not praise recklessness, his voyage was an exception. How the scene has changed!

Chronology of some firsts and records

1661   First known yacht race in England (between King Charles II and his brother, the Duke of York)

1720   Archives show Water Club of Cork exists (now Royal Cork Yacht Club, Crosshaven, Ireland)

1775   Cumberland Fleet races on Thames in London

1783   First ever steam boat (paddle wheeler)

1800   Probably no vessel, however propelled on water, had exceeded 10 knots

1815   Formation of 'The Yacht Club'; first ever use of such a phrase (now Royal Yacht Squadron, Cowes, England)

1826   First race for a cup at Cowes

1844   Formation of New York Yacht Club

1854   *Champion of the Seas*, Black Ball sailing liner, claims 19.5 knots

1855   Start of clipper ship period of about 25 years

1864   *Adelaide*, sailing freighter, New York to Liverpool in 12d 8h

1864   First motor boat with internal combustion engine

1887   First one-design racing class formed in Dublin (Waterwags)

1893   *Satanita*, 131ft cutter, reaches at 17 knots

1893   *Britannia*, royal cutter, similar size, averages 11.5 knots across English Channel and return

1905   *Atlantic*, schooner, New York to Lizard Point, record at 10.01 knots; record will stand for 75 years

1906   First transpacific yacht race

1912   First power boat timed at over 50 mph

1925   First Fastnet race; speed of first home: 4.26 knots

1928   *Miss America VII*, speed boat, timed at 92.9 mph

1931   *Dorade*, crack ocean racer, wins transatlantic race at average 6.93 knots

1933   Uffa Fox on International Canoe class boat timed at 16.3 knots

1938   Class A ice yacht timed at 125mph

1939   *Bluebird*, Sir Malcolm Campbell, world water speed record at 141.7mph

Second World War and subsequent recovery curtailed more extreme boating while regular racing and design recovered. However, war stimulated new materials and technical advance.

1959 Rudy Choy in *Aikane*, multihull, claims 12.7 knots over 24-hour period

1960 First Plymouth to Newport, RI, single-handed race, average of first home: 3.09 knots

1967 First single-handed one-stop circumnavigation of the world, *Gipsy Moth IV*

1969 First single-handed non-stop circumnavigation of the world, *Suhaili*

1970 Tornado class catamaran timed over 350 metres at 16.4 knots

1971 Maxi yacht *Windward Passage* Miami to Montego Bay race at 10.72 knots

1972 Eric Tabarly, single-handed, Plymouth to Newport, RI, at average 5.6 knots

1978 Current world water speed record by *Spirit of Australia* achieved at 317.2mph

1978 Chay Blyth and crew in multihull round Britain and Ireland at 6.2 knots

1980 Eric Tabarly in foiler *Paul Ricard* breaks 1905 transatlantic record at 11.93 knots

1980 *Crossbow II* timed over 500 metres at 36 knots

1980 Sailboard of Dirk Thijs, Hawaii, timed at 24.63 knots

1982 Jon Sanders sails single-handed non-stop three times round the world

1988 First single-handed non-stop circumnavigation of world by a woman

1989 First Vendée Globe race; first home *Ecureuil d'Aquitaine* at 8.29 knots

1990 *Jet Services V* transatlantic record, still standing, at 18.62 knots

1991 Fastest offshore passage ever made from Marseille to Carthage; *Pierre 1er*, multihull at 20.66 knots

1993 *Commodore Explorer*, multihull, circumnavigates world in less than 80 days thus winning Jules Verne Trophy

1993 *Yellow Pages* at 46.52 knots over 500 metres; highest speed of any sailing vessel ever timed

1994 *Lakota*, multihull, record around Britain and Ireland at 12.67 knots

1994 Laurent Bourgnon, single-handed transatlantic record in *Primagaz*, multihull, 7d 2h 34m (17.15 knots). Also takes single-handed (still stands) 24-hour distance run, 540.0 miles

1997 *Sport Elec*, crewed multihull, record around the world in 71d 14h

2001 Fourth Vendée Globe race: PRB, single-handed monohull, best time at 9.73 knots, 93d 3h 57m

2001 *PlayStation* breaks 11-year transatlantic record: 4d 17h 28m 6s (25.78 knots). On the same voyage she breaks the 24-hour record: 687.17 miles (28.63 knots)

It is not possible to start listing all the unusual craft which have crossed the Atlantic, but in 1995 an otherwise conventional yacht sailed across without a mast. In her 24ft (7.3m) *Jeanneau* one-design, Nicole van de Kerchove used only kites, of which a selection of designs was carried, to track from the Canaries to Guadeloupe in 28 days.

Other superlatives

First one-design classes

There are probably about 800 one-design classes in the world, if one counts classes with at least some form of racing structure and disregards those which are simply production series. The first in England was the Solent One-Design, whose first race was held in April 1896. It was a 33ft 3in (10.13m) keel boat with cabin, a bowsprit extending 6ft (1.82m), gaff cutter rigged with topsail. Ten were built initially by White Brothers, Itchen, Southampton. Up to twenty raced in the Solent in the 1900s, but the class dispersed after 1914.

The oldest English one-design still racing today is the Yorkshire One-Design (Royal Yorkshire Yacht Club). There were earlier one-design classes in Ireland and the USA: the Waterwag of Dublin (1887) and the North Haven dinghy of Penobscot Bay, Maine (1885), versions of which still sail.

The Waterwag changed in 1900 from the original 13ft (3.9m) boat to today's 14ft 3in (4.27m) dinghy designed by Mamie Doyle. It claims to be older than the American boat, which was really only a locally built wooden boat, each one fashioned in a similar way by eye, and not a one-design until 1920, when the lines were established. A batch of one-designs called the Herreshoff 15 was built for members of the Beverly Yacht Club in time to race for the 1899 season.

Biggest number of starters

Records of competitor numbers should always be judged by *starters*; not entries, which are just paper, nor finishers. The world's largest number of starters remains the contingent of 2072 boats which started on 21 June in the 1984 annual Danish Sjaelland Rundt (Round Seeland); this goes around many islands of Denmark in relatively sheltered conditions. Nowadays it has about 1100 starters each year.

There are some events in the Mediterranean which are growing in size each year and one of these might well exceed the record in the early 2000s.

In England, there is the annual Round the Island (Wight) race run by the Island Sailing Club, Cowes (see records for this course in Chapter 5).

Boasts are invariably made about its size, but it peaked in the boom year of 1989 at 1781, and numbers fell fairly steadily thereafter. There are now between about 1200 and 1800 each time. The oldest owner/skipper may have been Owen Aisher aged 91, a consistent competitor. In all these cases remember that each extra entry at such size levels is less committed, less skilled and less used to racing. All these are ballasted yachts and multihulls, not centreboard dinghies.

America's Cup facts

Until 1983, the New York Yacht Club's successful defence of the America's Cup was the longest unbroken winning run (since 1871) in any sport. The greatest number of consecutive wins by any *challenger* is now five by *Team New Zealand* in 1995; before that it was three by *Australia II* in 1983. Between 1871 and 1920, no challenger won a single race. The only skippers to have sailed in three or more stagings of the event are Charlie Barr, Harold S Vanderbilt and Dennis Conner (all USA). No country has won the cup unless that nation has been a contender in at least three consecutive cup series.

The closest finish was on 4 October 1901, when Sir Thomas Lipton's *Shamrock II* was timed at the finish two seconds ahead of *Columbia* sailed by Charlie Barr. The latter won on time allowance. The biggest (length overall) ever competitor was the American 1903 defender *Reliance*. She was 143ft 8in (41.4m) with a sail area of 16160 square feet (1500sq m), the biggest sail ever set on a single mast. Even her designer, Nathanael Herreshoff, said she was a freak; the rules were changed before the next contest.

Same boat/skipper, furthest north and south

Strangely, this is quite often quoted, though documentation is difficult. The achievement is to make the highest latitude both north and south (maximum latitude span). *Northern Light*, 40ft (12.2m), a steel copy of Moitessier's *Joshua*, sailed by Rolf Bjelke (Swe) and Deborah Shapiro (USA) sailed 'up and down' the world instead of 'around'. To the north, she reached Svalbard Island (80 degrees 29 minutes north) in August 1982, only stopping when blocked by ice on three sides. South, they sailed to Adelaide Island (66 degrees 45 minutes south).

Robin Knox-Johnston (Gbr) in *Suhaili* sailed on voyages to Mikis Fjord, Greenland (68 degrees 23 minutes north) and Cape Horn (55 degrees 59 minutes south). Others may have sailed beyond all these points, but seldom in the same boat north and south.

Longevity of rating rules

This book has concentrated on pure records, ignoring handicaps and ratings. Such rules are numerous and come and go in various parts of the world. However, there is one which remains in regular use, albeit for a relatively small number of racing yachts, and it is called simply the (ISAF) International Rule. It was created in 1906 by conferences in London, Paris and Berlin and an agreement among a few European countries. The boats resulting are keeled day racers: 6-metres, 8-metres and 12-metres (as used for some years in the America's Cup). In the past there were 23, 15, 10 and 7-metre boats. The formula and supported regulations have changed considerably over the years, but not unrecognizably. No other formula or handicap rule approaches this.

Smallest

There is a steady trickle of people who plan to 'sail around the world in the smallest possible boat'. Yachting magazines receive regular correspondence on the lines: 'I am well advanced with my plan for sailing non-stop around the world in the smallest yacht ever to do so. Please inform me of the smallest craft which has completed such a voyage.' Readers of this book will by now understand that this is 'information of a negative', because one cannot say if something smaller did not make it.

Meanwhile the practicality is that there are minimum amounts of stores and spares (assuming water can be made) which limit lower sizes. Few of these plans materialize. Probably *Suhaili* with Robin Knox-Johnston remains the smallest non-stop at 32ft 5in (9.75m). A circumnavigation with stops from the east coast of England and return, was made between 1972 and 1980 by the Caprice class bilge keel sloop *Super Shrimp*, 18ft 4in (5.6m), sailed by Shane Acton (Gbr) and his girlfriend.

Some very small sailing craft have made long voyages, other than a circumnavigation. In 1993 a transatlantic voyage was completed by the 5ft 4½in (1.64m) *Vera Hugh Pride of Merseyside* (how did he find room to write the name?) sailed, single-handed of course, by Tom McNally (Gbr). He started from Sagres, Portugal, and after a collision with a ro-ro ferry sailed on to Madeira and then San Juan, Puerto Rico.

On the way he was seriously ill with a glandular complaint. He then sailed on to Fort Lauderdale, Florida, totalling 139 days at sea. He managed to take this 'record' from a kind of barrel with twin running headsails called

Small – smallest? The fringe (!) can be relied on to attempt oceans in ever smaller 'yachts'. This is a successful Atlantic crosser, Tom McClean in the 7ft 9¾in (2.37m) Giltspur.

Toniky-Nou, 5ft 10½in (1.79m), in which Eric Peters (Gbr) sailed from Las Palmas to Guadeloupe in 46 days in 1983.

Other Atlantic crossings had been made by Tom McClean (Gbr) twice, the second time in the 7ft 9¾in (2.37m) *Giltspur*, and by Hugh Vihlen (USA) in *April Fool*, 6ft 0in (1.83m), in 1968. But Vihlen turned up at Falmouth having taken 104 days from Nova Scotia in a 'boat' he said measured half an inch less than McNally: the outcome is unrecorded!

Inevitably there have been losses, some probably unreported: John Riding (Gbr) in *Sjo Ag* (Sea Egg), 12ft 0in (3.66m), crossed the Atlantic successfully, but later disappeared when attempting the Pacific.

The earliest known 'Tiny' (This Is Not Yachting) attempt was in 1888 when the 12ft 9in (3.90m) *Dark Secret*, sailed single-handed by William Andrews (USA), left Boston for England; he was taken off at sea by a Norwegian sailing barque after 62 days.

The Pacific was crossed in 1981 from Long Beach, California, to Sydney, New South Wales, by Gerry Spiess (USA), again obviously alone, in the 10ft 0in (3.05m) *Yankee Girl*. Perhaps the greatest reward of the diminutive is held by the Australian Serge Testa, who in the 11ft 10in (3.60m) *Acrohc Australis* circumnavigated the world by a tropical route from Brisbane, Queensland, and back between 1984 and 1987, calling at a number of ports.

Most consistent high sailing speed

This rather awkward heading is used to mention the recent (1999–2000) arrival of very big multihulls designed and built for 'The Race/Course du Millénaire'. No upper limit or configuration was set. The boats were allowed to be machines of any size, so long as they were propelled by sail. However, when they appeared at the start line off Barcelona, Spain, all turned out to be catamarans and all were quite close in overall length. Earlier in this book will be found records that one or other has beaten, but sailing vessels have never before sailed at such consistent high speeds, though this is not practicable to quantify.

ClubMed (Fra/Nzl) was 110ft (33.50m), beam 54ft (16.50m) and built like most of the others by sandwich carbon – Nomex. *PlayStation* (USA) was built in New Zealand then rebuilt in England to an extended length of 125ft (38.1m). The other comparable vessels in 2000 were *Warta Polpharma* (Pol), *Team Legato* (Gbr), *Team Adventure* (USA) and *Innovation Explorer* (Fra).

Yacht clubs: largest, oldest, richest

When considering the statistics of yacht and sailing clubs and associations, we are on less certain ground, for figures have to depend on those supplied by the clubs themselves.

The best claimant for a genuine club in terms of the number of members is the Argentinian Club Nautico San Isidro with 'slightly over 10000 members'. It is located on two islands at the beginning of the Rio de la Plata and covers 6 million square metres. This club has 4 restaurants, a snack bar, a library, several meeting rooms, 10 tennis courts, an 18-hole golf course, and its own boatyard and sailing school; 450 yachts owned by members are berthed there, the club itself owning 90 dinghies, mainly Optimists. There is also a large steel ketch which makes ocean voyages.

Second comes the Royal Hong Kong Yacht Club, whose name was the cause of major political debate before the then colony became part of mainland China. In the end it kept the 'Royal' in the name (as with clubs in the republics of Ireland, South Africa, Malta and elsewhere), but the crown was removed from all insignia. The Royal Hong Kong has about 8000 members, a massive clubhouse, swimming pool and boat area. Third is a club without a dedicated clubhouse, the (British) Royal Naval Sailing Association: it has 7200 members around the world, but one suspects a declining membership albeit a particular active one in serious cruising and racing.

In Japan, the Nippon Ocean Racing Club has nearly 6000 members and is at various stations around this hugely populated country of strong maritime traditions. By convention the royal title is never used for Japanese clubs.

The Cruising Association with a purpose built clubhouse in London has 5000 members.

Many 'top of the range' clubs have membership of between 800 and 1800: these include the Yacht Club de France (1500), the Cruising Yacht Club of Australia (1500) and San Diego (California) Yacht Club (1800).

Among exclusive clubs which limit the size of their membership are the Seawanhaka Corinthian YC of Oyster Bay, NY, with 450, the Royal Cruising Club (Gbr: no clubhouse) with 400, Larchmont YC, Long Island Sound (USA) (600), and the Royal Yacht Squadron, Cowes, Isle of Wight, 450, all male.

As for the *oldest yacht club*, claims of various sorts are often made, but I have researched the possibilities and reached sound conclusions. A particular claimant is the Royal Cork Yacht Club, Crosshaven, Co Cork, Ireland. Its history is based on the documentation and paintings describing the activities of the Water Club of the Harbour of Cork as early as 1720: processions of small sailing vessels, dinners and so on. The British Admiralty had granted a special ensign in 1759; the club headquarters were at Haulbowline Island. However, after some years, probably owing to the

Napoleonic Wars, it faded from view. When the Cork Yacht Club (later 'Royal') was formed in 1828, members of the Water Club joined it and ancestry was claimed.

In 1870, another club, the Royal Munster YC, was formed over the water at Crosshaven, while the Royal Cork clubhouse was in Cobh. In 1968 the clubs amalgamated and moved into the Royal Munster clubhouse with the name Royal Cork.

In 1772, the Starcross Club (not 'yacht', not 'sailing') was founded at Starcross, South Devon. A 'fête marine', probably not its first, held on 11 August 1775, included sailing processions, rowing events, cannons fired, fireworks, dinners and balls for the gentry, as well as a day off for the locals. At some stage in the early nineteenth century (again those wars were in the interval) the Starcross Yacht Club was formed, splitting away from the original club which had become more of a village carnival.

In 1749 the Prince of Wales (later King George III) gave a cup to be competed for by 12 yachts racing on the Thames in London. Then from 1775 until 1782, his brother the Duke of Cumberland gave an annual cup, and the boats involved formed the Cumberland Sailing Society, which had uniforms and a commodore. The latter led the fleet to its moorings after the race and was the origin of the term in English yachting ('commodore' is used in Anglo-Saxon countries, but on the Continent the senior person is the 'president').

In 1823 there was a dispute in the club and some members broke away to form the Thames Yacht Club. In 1830, this became the Royal Thames Yacht Club which has been active in yachting and yacht racing to this day. The Cumberland Sailing Society, which had been re-named, disappeared. On this basis the Royal Thames YC claims it was founded in 1775.

Only one club which claims to be oldest can show a pedigree of total continuity, without a day missed, and displaying unwavering purpose. That is the club that was formed on 1 June 1815, when 42 gentlemen, about half of them titled, met at the Thatched House Tavern, St James's, London. The club they started was simply called 'The Yacht Club'. Such a term had never been heard before, though thousands have copied it since. In September the Prince Regent joined. In 1820 he became George IV and the name of the club was changed to the Royal Yacht Club.

In 1833, King William IV declared that he was graciously pleased to consider himself the head of the club, which should henceforth be known as the Royal Yacht Squadron. It always met in Cowes every August; on 6 July 1858 it moved into West Cowes Castle, where it has remained ever since.

Land yachts, such as those of the DN class seen here, currently achieve speeds in excess of 65mph.

Ice yachts and land yachts

The accepted dates for the origin of effective sailing land craft are 1543 for the first land yacht and 1790 for the first ice yacht. Ice yachts are the fastest of all machines under sail, because of the minimal friction of ice just as in figure skating, ice hockey and other ice borne sports. Because, assuming reasonable wind strength, the speed rapidly picks up, ice yachts are invariably close-hauled. The same circumstances apply to land yachts, and speeds are improved as better wheel bearings and other moving parts are developed.

The most widely sailed class of ice yacht is the DN (long ago originated by the *Detroit News*), which frequently achieves speeds of 55 to 65 knots. Speed trials are not undertaken by the class authorities, because of technical difficulties; nor is there any particular incentive. Under class rules the DN has a LOA of 12ft 3in (3.73m), beam of 1ft 9in (0.54m). There is a single (main)sail with luff length 14ft (4.26m) and foot just under 9ft (2.7m). Ice yachts, of course, do not 'float': they have 'runners'; these are a maximum length of 2ft 6in (0.76m).

There is a larger class, the E-Skeeter with 183 square feet (17.0sq m) of sail. Now accepted as the largest ever ice yacht was a gaff rigged sloop called *Icicle* which had a length of 70ft (21.0m). She existed in the 1860s, was built for John E Roosevelt (USA) and was based at Poughkeepsie on the upper Hudson River, NY. The fastest recorded speed (distance, timing arrangements and suchlike not known) is believed to have been in 1938 by John Buckstaff (USA) who achieved 143mph or 123 knots in what was then called a class A stern steerer on Lake Winnebago, Wisconsin.

Land yachts also had a DN class similar to the ice DN, but with wheels. Classes have been developed which are rated by size: mainly the sail area figure. The recognized outright land yacht speed record is 66.5mph or 57.8 knots. This was achieved in March 1981 by Christian-Yves Nau (Fra) in the vehicle *Mobil*, in severe gale conditions at Le Touquet, France.

9

Power boat records

By the time the commercial sailing ships had reached the best speeds ever achieved in the second half of the nineteenth century, mechanically propelled ships and boats had been in existence for nearly 100 years. For some time one was as likely to see a sailing vessel as a steamer on the high seas and in coastal waters; only after 1914 did wide use of sail greatly diminish.

Mechanical ship firsts

The first steam driven boat appeared in 1783, a 138ft (42.1m) wooden paddle wheeler, *Pyroscaphe*, which plied on the River Saône between Lyon and Ile Barbe. She had been built by the Marquis de Joffrey d'Abbans (Fra).

The world's first screw driven vessel was built to the order of Colonel John Stevens (USA) and was the 25ft (7.6m) *Little Juliana* with twin four-bladed propellers and a speed of 7 knots. Stevens went further, and in 1809 was responsible for the first voyage at sea by a mechanical vessel: the 95-ton *Phoenix* which went from New York to Philadelphia in fine mid-summer.

This chapter looks at 'power boats', by which is meant speed or race-dedicated boats of less than 150ft (45.7m). This dimension is the internationally accepted cut off measurement, though most activities involve boat lengths some way below the figure. The first petrol driven motor boat was built by Gottlieb Daimler (Ger) at Canstatt, Germany and ran on the River Neckar in August 1866. The first regular commercial production was at Putney by the River Thames in England in 1893, Daimler engines being fitted to river launches which had previously been rowed and sailed.

The first motor boat race was held at the Royal Cork Yacht Club, Queenstown, Ireland, in 1903. It was for the Harmsworth Trophy and was won by a 75hp Napier engined launch at 19.5mph. Interestingly this was designed by Linton Hope, better known for his racing yachts. The first 'hydroplane', meaning then, in effect, a small speedboat with a stepped hull, appeared in 1914.

World outright water speed records: same progressive times

DATE	BOAT	DRIVER	NAT	PLACE	SPEED mph
1903	Napier	S F Edge	GBR	Cork	24.9
1928	Miss America VII	Gar Wood	USA	Detroit	92.9
1932	Miss England III	Kaye Don	GBR	Loch Lomond	117.43
1932	Miss America X	Gar Wood	USA	Detroit	124.9
1939	Bluebird	Sir Malcolm Campbell	GBR	Lake Coniston	141.7
1952	Slo-Mo-Shun IV	Stanley Sayres	USA	Lake Washington	178.5
1955	Bluebird	Donald Campbell	GBR	Nevada	216.3
1964	Bluebird	Donald Campbell	GBR	Lake Coniston	260.3
1978	Spirit of Australia	Ken Warby	AUS	Blowering Dam	317.19

Here are some of the world water speed records (under power) of the twentieth century. There have been intermediate ones, especially in the Miss America and Miss England period, but the table shows how water speed advanced. There were no such recordings before the twentieth century and, so far, no improvement since.

Greatest speed on water

At first the Harmsworth Trophy was where the fastest boats were to be found. By 1914 speeds were up to 50mph (mph rather than knots tended to be used in power); by 1931 they reached 100mph. Before this it became apparent that any attempt on the world water speed record could not be achieved in the chopped up water and predetermined start time of a race (as we have seen in sailing) and a suitable flat water location and calm weather were prerequisites.

In 1932, *Miss England III* driven by Kaye Don (Gbr) on Loch Lomond, Scotland, recorded 117.43mph. Within months this was beaten by *Miss America X* (USA) driven by Gar Wood off Detroit at 124.9mph.

So it went on, with boats and drivers exclusively from Great Britain and the United States, as the list shows. Up to 1939, the American boats always had a Packard engine and the British had a Rolls Royce aero engine. Later there were Westinghouse (USA) and Metropolitan–Vickers Beryl (Gbr) engines.

Then for the first time came a new nationality, the present holder, the Australian Ken Warby. In 1978, at the age of 39, he recorded 317.19 mph at Blowering Dam, Australia in *Spirit of Australia*, a vessel powered with a Westinghouse J-34 turbo jet engine.

Over the years the casualty toll in this field was never light; unfortunately there is a considerable list including the British 'speed kings' Sir Henry Segrave (1930), John Cobb (1952) and Donald Campbell (1967).

The world outright record requires a long, expensive and highly organized campaign, but there are many other records now well categorized by boat and engine size, distance, time and over specific courses. The authority for these is the Union Internationale Motonautique (UIM), long established in Monaco. UIM currently has one world record per class and this can be run over a nautical mile, a statute mile or a kilometre. There are numerous rules including those on timing arrangements and tolerances; two runs, one in each direction, are always required: this is known simply as *speed*. There are distance records (best time for the distance) but, unlike sailing, these are taken over closed courses; in other words, round and round the same buoys. Then there are 1 hour, 2 hour, etc duration records up to 12 and 24 hours: in this case it is the best distance achieved in the set time. The types of craft (actual class) fall under one of these headings: all UIM series and classes; American Powerboat Association classes; prototypes. As this is a book about records, detail of classes is not included here, but some of their speeds are notable. Current speed records for some UIM classes:

> **Class I and II offshore** 1999, D Allenby (Gbr) 109.3mph
> **Class III offshore 6-litre** 1998, B Warelius (Fin) 116.4mph
> **Class 0.700** 1997, J Sean McKean, (USA) 122.0mph
> **Class R. Unlimited** 1997, J Noone (Gbr) 145.5mph
> **Class Formula 1** 1999, A Marshall (Gbr) 136.7mph
> **Class Unlimited immersed propeller** 1962, R Duby (USA) 200.4mph

Note that all the above are *speed* as technically described above. The distance, 1 hour, etc, and endurance speeds are for every class slower figures than 'speed' trials. The categories and classes do mean that there are a large number of prizes and records: about 210 such names and figures for the 1999 list of UIM.

Passage records

As with sailing, passage records have become established over the years, based on traditional regular races or simply routes that lend themselves to a port-to-port run. With power boats, the need to refuel arises unless the distance is very short. Among rules governing this are a prohibition of re-fuelling at sea with some specially arranged tender; the reasons against this include the very high expense and the likelihood of spillage. Therefore, vessels must put into port. This is like a 'pitstop' and the clock continues to run.

This aspect of power boating is fairly new and is being pioneered from Great Britain. Some of the rules are based, as far as applicable to power, on those of the WSSRC. This applies to definitions of 'non-stop' and 'stopping', but the former cannot work beyond a certain distance because of the fuel need described.

The common power boat route is not around Britain and Ireland, which is open sea and convenient under sail, but round the mainland of Great Britain only (England, Wales, Scotland). Assumed distance is 1568 statute miles or 1380 nautical miles. The holder dates from July 1992 and is *Drambuie Tantalus* (Gbr), 50ft (15.2m), a 'scarab' monohull driven by four 650hp Caterpillar diesel engines: she took 1d 20h 3m 30s, an average of 35.60mph or 31.33 knots. (Best speed sailing round Britain and Ireland is 12.67 knots.)

An under 30ft (9.14m) category was created and resulted in 2d 15h 32m 25s by a Rapier 29, 29ft (8.8m), powered by one 240hp Yamaha diesel in July 1992. The crew were Metropolitan (London) police skippered by Steve Brownridge. Their average speed was 21.70 knots. Recently a route which is the same as the sailing course round Britain and Ireland has been established for individual attempts.

The London to Monte Carlo, Monaco, race of 2947 statute miles was first run in 1972, the original event having 14 stops. It is now rerouted at 2392 miles, as an individually attempted run; the current record holder is Dr Rolf Versen (Ger) in a Hanse Werte, Bremerhaven, hull with two 600hp Man diesels. The time was 3d 17h 18m 17s with average speed of 26.78 mph or 23.57 knots.

Two shorter distances from England are given below. The short time required means weather (calm or very light wind) can be chosen with accuracy and higher speeds attained.

Shorter routes starting in England

Poole, south coast of England, to Cherbourg, north coast of France; 71.9 statute miles; 63.3 nautical miles. The record is held by Mark Pascoe (Gbr) in *Vulture Ventures*, 52m 21s (82.42mph or 72.53 knots).

Around the Isle of Wight (compare sailing records, fastest 19.53 knots); 56.8 statute miles (50 nautical miles) Record holders: John and Richard Puddifoot (Gbr) in unlimited class, but also classified as RIB Formula 1, rounded in 43m 48s, 78.82mph, 66.79 knots.

Round the world

A 60ft (18.3m) powered trimaran called *Cable & Wireless Adventurer* (Gbr) was specially designed by Nigel Irens to make an individual world circumnavigation record, starting from Gibraltar in April 1998. Built by Vosper Thornycroft, Southampton, England, she had Cummins diesels and was capable of 50 knots. The skipper was Ian Bosworth accompanied by John Walker and crew. The route was via the Suez and Panama Canals with numerous refuelling stops and some wandering around for sponsorship purposes.

The UIM recognized a world circumnavigation record of 74 days 20 hours 58 minutes 30 seconds. The UIM gives the distance as 24382 nautical miles and average resulting speed 13.74 knots. Starting and finishing dates at Gibraltar were 19 April 1998 and 3 July 1998.

If the vessel did enter the southern hemisphere it was not far beyond the equator, with Malé to Singapore being one of the legs. This was an outstanding feat and will not often be imitated, so it has been inevitable that any rules are to some extent devised to fit what, in practice, is seen to be achieved.

It is possible for a vessel without sails to circumnavigate quickly without stopping, but it has to be a rather special ship. One supposes that it could be done by a modern cruise liner, by leaving its passengers ashore, making any necessary mechanical adjustments and then filling up with sufficient fuel for the whole trip. But this has never happened and is unlikely, because for a commercial shipping line there is no benefit in it of any sort, except perhaps the publicity of an achievement which would be understood by very few. But it would be an admirable 28-day wonder (28 days is a guess).

A warship is more likely, and a nuclear powered vessel would have no refuelling problems. This is exactly what happened with one claimant, the submarine USS *Triton* (Captain Edward L Beach USN), which sailed from New London, Connecticut, on 16 February 1960, remained submerged and returned there 83 days later.

In 1999, I was contacted by Captain J A Hamilton, a retired British merchant marine officer, who claimed that many years before, the MV *Benwyvis* had steamed around the world non-stop crossing her outward track in 73 days.

It is a satisfying fact in this modern age that the non-stop circumnavigation is now faster under sail and the time of 71 days 14 hours, at the time of writing, is likely to be improved. Improved power records, stopping and non-stopping, will depend on incentives and rewards rather than technical potential which is itself considerable.

9

Records to go for

Among the world's sailing and some power records which have been surveyed, it is remarkable how many are recent ones. At present, there are very few records which were set prior to 1991; over 30 per cent are post-1995.

In recent years the speed range for sailing on water has seen major advances. The reason for this lies in the building and structural materials available, including the underlying chemical-aided techniques for hulls, rigs and sails.

Offshore electronic communications and navigation have enabled vessels to select routeing for weather and other advantages with precision. Thus seeking records, both individually attempted and in a regular event, has become a well supported branch of yacht racing.

Favourites

Although there are more than 100 sailing records listed by WSSRC and hundreds more which may be pursued locally, this chapter lists some of the potential record breakers:

- A sponsor wanting to enter record breaking
- A new boat, claiming to be fastest of its type is launched
- Trials before a scheduled international race

These records may be 'classic', or vulnerable, or just more practical than others. Remember that as well as the outright best time, there are records for the single-hander, all-female crew and the monohull.

What follows mentions the route and makes comment, even if this may repeat what has been covered in earlier chapters. For the current holder and exact record time, see earlier in this book, or refer to publications given in the appendix.

Inshore 500-metre run

At almost any given moment there are several projects in different parts of the world developing craft to beat the world's outright speed record. This has to be on a 500-metre one-way run, or at least it has been for the last 30 years. It needs to be single-minded, properly financed and have a suitable location with good wind (strength and direction) and smooth water likely. This will be a canal type section, lake with flat hinterland or sheltered coast with depth of water really close to shore. A location which just happens to be near the building site or in the country of origin is not sufficient today. There is probably a maximum that can be sailed, or at least where increments get smaller and smaller.

Among the list of classes for the 500-metre run, the *10 square metre class* level is important. So far this has suited boards. A faster board is a possibility, though they have gone quiet since the early 1990s.

Offshore distance

Best distance in 24 hours is fortuitous. In other words, it invariably occurs during the course of a long passage, maybe in the Southern Ocean, the North Atlantic, or trade winds. With a suitable vessel (which for the outright now has to be a large multihull), proper arrangements must be set up in advance for shore reception of data, as described earlier. Any 24-hour period is acceptable or shorter, but never longer.

Circumnavigation: 21600 miles

'Round the world in eighty days' has long been beaten. A large multihull looks to be the way forward, but do not disregard a specially designed monohull, even for outright and certainly for mono, if that is attractive. The closer to the Antarctic, the shorter is the great circle/rhumb line distance. The WSSRC record is not necessarily the same as the Jules Verne, but combining the two is an accepted option. A start in the southern hemisphere is another option. WSSRC rules allow choice of start point (which has also to be the finish point).

Pacific Ocean

New York to San Francisco via Cape Horn
This very long route (13208 miles) is one of the major passages even to achieve; to hold the record is outstanding. The list of skippers is a short and select roll of historic voyagers.

There is now a race organized on the route, but individual attempts have also been usual. It has to be made in the southern hemisphere summer, though it may be snowing in New York. Isabelle Autissier was trapped by pack ice at the tip of Manhattan when trying to leave in February 1994 and had to be freed by a fire boat. She then started a few days later.

Transpacific routes

These are the ones to go for in the case of a yacht based on the Pacific rim or taking part in various races in those waters. They are not too often attempted, so there is a higher chance of beating the record. They should all be made in the northern hemisphere summer. Starting on the coast of California:

Los Angeles to Honolulu, Hawaii
This 2224-mile course is the long-established Transpac race. The trade wind is invariably fair and fresh. Multihulls should go for individual attempts against race and individual records. The record breaker should attempt this as part of a circuit.

Honolulu to Yokohama, Japan, east to west
This course is 3750 miles; the weather systems are favourable. Then yachts sail back without stopping for:

Yokohama to San Francisco, west to east
This course is 4525 miles.

Australian waters

The Sydney to Hobart race: 615 miles
Starting every Boxing Day this race has its own best time on record. WSSRC policy invites individual attempts over classic race routes. This is one that should certainly be attempted and an individual on a weather window could beat the race time. Other major Australian races can be

looked at in the same way, but there is no current basis to mention as comparison. In other words, there have been particular successive attempts.

Round Australia: 7500 miles
This is always there for an individual record: at present it looks a practical one to beat.

Atlantic Ocean

New York to Lizard Point record: 2925 miles
This record was unbroken for 75 years and was then unbroken between 1988 and 2001. It remains open to an ever-quicker passage and will always be a favourite, if not 'the classic'. America to England across the gale-wracked northern North Atlantic has an eternal attraction for speed sailors. All the different categories are particularly acclaimed on this route. Even the power boats eye it (though they used to finish at Bishop Rock, some distance short).

Cadiz, Spain, to San Salvador (Watling Island): 3884 miles
This is the trade wind route in the North Atlantic. Originally a race in 1992 to celebrate the five hundredth anniversary of the first Atlantic voyage of Christopher Columbus, it is now a route for individual attempts. It has sure sunshine with steady wind direction and high speeds are possible. Races are sometimes run on the general direction of the route, but with other and varying start (in Europe) and finish (in Caribbean) points. These races cannot better the individual attempt on the approved route.

US east coast

Miami to New York: 947 miles
This is a convenient route close to important yachting bases. The distance is potentially a fast one, as a weather window can be selected for the whole passage. It is a useful route for a vessel which then intends to stand by for New York to Lizard Point.

Newport, RI, to Bermuda: 615 miles
This is sailed by the biennial race for conventional ocean racers. Other races, two-handed, multis and such like are also organized and may be faster, but once again the individual attempt may beat any race and has the yacht-friendly starting base of Newport.

From a time of six days, Loïck Peyron and crew in Fujicolor II, *in a time of 1 day 16 hours and 27 minutes, almost reduced the 605-mile Fastnet race to a 'day sail'.*

Europe

Among the fairly numerous routes in European waters, the following can probably always be improved upon.

Marseille to Carthage, Tunisia: 458 miles

This is potentially the fastest of all routes. It will be sailed when the Mistral is blowing and it can blow for the whole straight line sail. Particularly applicable to different categories; with the latest multihulls and even monos, it takes less than 24 hours.

Fastnet race: 605 miles

Vessels stand by in a main yachting base for this race; the route is from Cowes, Isle of Wight, to the Fastnet rock and finishes at Plymouth, south-west England. The record may be that of the race, which in recent years has permitted multihulls. There have been a few individual attempts and it remains quite practical to beat the race record.

Round Britain and Ireland: 1787 miles

As with any 'circular' or closed loop route, fast times are difficult. The wind will not be consistent and the length of course means weather changes beyond a reasonable forecast period. Any WSSRC agreed start/finish point is acceptable. The months from November to March inclusive are not advisable, owing to long hours of darkness (close to 61 degrees north) and winter storm conditions in the northern extremities of the route.

Round the Isle of Wight: 50 miles

Back now to where we started, on a short sprint near a coastline. It was where the schooner *America*, carrying the burgee of the New York Yacht Club, won a race on 22 August 1851; but she did not sail very fast, just rather faster than her British rivals. Since then many a record time has been clocked, using all sorts of criteria.

This surely fits the description of the 'traditional route'. It is difficult to put up a time as fast as, say, Marseille to Carthage, for, though short and well within theoretical weather window time, the tidal streams can never be fair all the way round this diamond-shaped piece of land. They can be taken fair on three sides though, but that timing may not fit the desired starting schedule for the weather.

Certainly individual attempts will beat the big annual race around (for the 'individual versus event' reasons earlier stated). There is no logistic problem for a vessel standing by for days, perhaps weeks, within a short sail of the start line just off the 'castle' of the Royal Yacht Squadron. The route can be taken in either direction. Open at any time, summer or winter, to the sailing speed machines of the world, potentially near to spectators for all its way, this is a record passage which can be broken again and again for many years to come.

Summary of the recommended records to beat

- 500-metre one-way outright
- 500-metre in 10 square metre class
- Best distance in 24 hours
- New York to San Francisco via Cape Horn
- Los Angeles to Honolulu
- Hawaii to Yokohama
- Yokohama to San Francisco
- Sydney to Hobart
- Round Australia
- Ambrose Light Tower to Lizard Point
- Cadiz to San Salvador (Watling Island)
- Miami to New York
- Newport to Bermuda
- Marseille to Carthage
- Fastnet
- Round Britain and Ireland
- Round the Isle of Wight

Appendix 1
Contacts and Addresses

For a listing of up-to-date records, current rules and notices of races where a record is within an event, readers should contact the appropriate organization. Here are some of those most involved.

The international authority

The website will lead to all national authorities, classes and other links and information.

International Sailing
Federation (ISAF),
Ariadne House,
Town Quay,
Southampton SO14 1AE
UK

website: www.sailing.org

Sailing records, listings, rules and application

World Sailing Speed Record
Council,
PO Box 2,
Bordon,
Hampshire GU35 6JX
UK

website: www.sailspeedrecords.com

Motor boat records, listings, rules and application

Union Internationale
Motonautique,
1 avenue des Castelans,
Stade Louis II, Entrée H,
MC 9000
Principality of Monaco

website: www.powerboating.com

Newport to Bermuda

Cruising Club of America,
c/o Truman S Casner, Secretary,
PO Box 4024,
Boston, MA 0201

e-mail: tcasner@ropesgray.com

Royal Bermuda Yacht Club,
Albuoy's Point,
Hamilton,
Bermuda

website: www.rbyc.bm

Sydney to Hobart and other courses

Cruising Yacht Club of Australia,
New Beach Road,
Darling Point,
2027 NSW,
Australia

website: www.cyca.com.au

Fastnet race and other courses

Royal Ocean Racing Club,
20 St James's Place,
London, SW1A 1NN

website: www.rorc.org

Appendix 2

WSSRC ratified passage records

Major outright and all other ratified records (speed order)

Race/Route	Distance Nm	Date	Yacht
Transatlantic W to E, Ambrose Light – Lizard Point	2925	Oct 01	*PlayStation*
Cowes – St Malo	138	Dec 01	*PlayStation*
Marseille – Carthage	458	Aug 91	*Pierre Ier*
Transpacific, Los Angeles – Honolulu	2215	Jul 97	*Explorer*
Round Ireland, non stop, crewed	708	Sep 93	*Lakota*
Round Britain and Ireland, all islands, non-stop, crewed	1787	Oct 94	*Lakota*
Round the World, non-stop, crewed, any type, Jules Verne Trophy	21760	Mar-May 97	*Sport Elec*
Transpacific W to E, Yokohama – San Francisco	4482	Aug 98	*Explorer*
New York – San Francisco, non-stop, crewed	13945	Feb 94	*Ecureuil Poitou Charentes*

Race/Route	Distance Nm	Date	Yacht
Round the Isle of Wight	50	Nov 01	*PlayStation*
Miami – New York	947	May 01	*PlayStation*
Transatlantic W to E, Ambrose Light – Lizard Point, singlehanded	2925	Jun 94	*Primagaz*
Newport, RI – Bermuda	635	Jan 00	*PlayStation*
Marseille – Carthage, monohull	458	Sep 98	*Stealth*
Cadiz – San Salvador	3884	Jun 00	*ClubMed*
Newport, RI – Bermuda, singlehanded	635	Jun 99	*Lakota*
Sydney – Hobart (annual race)	630	Dec 99	*Mari-Cha III*
Thailand Gulf	59	Mar 97	*Dermophil*
Transatlantic W to E, Ambrose Light – Lizard Point, monohull	2925	Feb 01	*Armor Lux-Foie Gas Bizac*
Transatlantic W to E, Ambrose Light – Lizard Point, all-women crew	2925	Jun 97	*Royal & Sun Alliance*
Newport – Bermuda (monohull)	635	Nov 96	*CCP/Cray Valley*
Transatlantic E to W, Plymouth – Newport singlehanded	2800	Jun 00	*Eure et Loire*
Round the Isle of Wight, monohull, westabout	50	Sep 93	*Dolphin and Youth*
Honolulu – Yokohama	3750	Aug 95	*Lakota*
Round the World, non stop, singlehanded, Vendée Globe	21760	Nov 00-Feb 01	*PRB*
Round the World, non stop, singlehanded, woman, Vendée Globe	21760	Nov 00-Feb 01	*Kingfisher*
Transpacific E to W, San Francisco – Yokohama	4482	May 96	*Lakota*
Plymouth – La Rochelle	355	May 01	*Netergy.com Challenge*
Transpacific W to E, Yokohama – San Francisco, singlehanded	4525	Aug 96	*Lakota*
Transatlantic E to W, Plymouth – Newport, monohull and woman any vessel	2800	Jun 00	*Kingfisher*
Dakar – Guadeloupe	2700	Feb 99	*Simac*
Round Britain and Ireland, all islands, non-stop, monohull	1787	Aug 00	*Sail That Dream*
Round Britain and Ireland, all islands, non-stop, women	1787	Aug 00	*Team Pindar*
Round the World, non stop, westabout, singlehanded	21760	Jan-Jun 00	*Uunet*
Round Britain and Ireland, all islands, non-stop, singlehanded	1787	Aug 00	*Zeal*
Round Ireland (singlehanded)	708	Oct 01	*Zeal*
Round the World, assisted, westabout, singlehanded, woman, stops	21760	Jul 96	*Heath Insured II*

Type	LOA ft / m		Owner/Skipper	Nationality	Elapsed Time	Average Speed Kn
C	125	38.1	Steve Fossett	USA	4d 17h 28m 6s	25.78
C	125	38.1	Steve Fossett	USA	6h 21m 54s	21.68
T	60	18.29	Florence Arthaud	FRA	22h 9m 56s	20.66
C	86	26.21	Bruno Peyron	FRA	5d 9h 18m 26s	17.21
T	60	18.29	Steve Fossett	USA	1d 20h 42m	15.84
T	60	18.29	Steve Fossett	USA	5d 21h 5m 27s	12.67
T	90	27.4	Olivier de Kersauson	FRA	71d 14h 22m 8s	12.66
C	85	25.91	Bruno Peyron & Skip Novak	FRA	14d 17h 22m 50s	12.56
S	60	18.29	Isabelle Autissier	FRA	63d 5h 55m	9.33
C	125	38.1	Steve Fossett	USA	2h 33m 55s	19.53
C	125	38.0	Steve Fossett	USA	2d 5h 54m 42s	17.57
T (I)	60	18.29	Laurent Bourgnon	FRA	7d 2h 34m 42s	17.15
C	105	32.0	Steve Fossett	USA	1d 14h 35m 53s	16.45
S	90	27.43	Giovanni Agnelli	ITA	1d 5h 2m 6s	15.77
C	110	33.50	Grant Dalton	NZL/FRA	10d 14h 53m 44s	15.23
T (I)	60	18.29	Steve Fossett	USA	1d 16h 51m 54s	15.05
S	147	44.7	Robert Miller	GBR	1d 18h 27m 10s	14.83
C	18	5.48	Mitch Booth & Herbert Derckson	USA	4h 8m 35s	14.24
S	60	18.29	Bernard Stamm	SUI	8d 20h 55m 35s	13.73
C	92	28.0	Tracy Edwards	GBR	9d 11h 21m 55s	12.87
S	50	15.24	Jean-Pierre Mouligne	FRA/USA	2d 5h 55m 55s	11.76
T(I)	60	18.29	Francis Joyon	FRA	9d 23h 54m 36s	11.67
S	64	19.05	Matthew Humphries	GBR	4h 21m 56s	11.36
T	60	18.29	Steve Fossett	USA	13d 20h 9m 22s	11.29
S (I)	60	18.29	Michel Desjoyeaux	FRA	93d 3h 57m 32s	9.73
S (I)	60	18.29	Ellen MacArthur	GBR	94d 4h 25m 40s	9.63
T	60	18.29	Steve Fossett	USA	19d 15h 18m 9s	9.51
T	40	12.19	Pete Berry	GBR	37h 33m 23s	9.46
T (I)	60	18.29	Steve Fossett	USA	20d 9h 52m 59s	9.24
S(I)	60	18.29	Ellen MacArthur	GBR	14d 23h 11m	7.79
C	19	5.79	Hans Bouscholte & Gerard Navarin	NED	15d 2h 26m 58s	7.45
S	50	15.24	Alex Thompson	GBR	10d 18h 27m 23s	6.91
S	50	15.24	Miranda Merron & Emma Richards	GBR	11d 6h 58m 17s	6.59
S(I)	60	18.29	Philippe Monnet	FRA	151d 19h 54m 36s	5.97
S(I)	38	11.58	Peter Keig	GBR	18d 13h 59m 59s	4.01
S	38	11.58	Peter Keig	GBR	7d 10h 24m 27s	3.96
S (I)	67	20.42	Samantha Brewster	GBR	247d 14h 51m 7s	3.66

Ocean race records

These times are of established and traditional race courses. They represent the best-ever elapsed time as confirmed by the race organizer

Race/Route	Distance Nm	Date	Yacht
Newport, CA – Ensenada	125	Feb 98	*Stars and Stripes*
San Diego – Puerto Vallarta	991	Feb 98	*Lakota*
Round the Isle of Wight (annual race)	50	Jun 01	*Dexia Eure et Loire*
The Race, Course du Millénaire	23300	Jan–Mar 01	*ClubMed*
Chicago – Mackinac	293	Jul 98	*Stars and Stripes*
Quebec – St Malo	2897	Jul 96	*Fujicolor II*
Transatlantic W to E, Ambrose Light – Lizard Point (monohull powered sails rule 5c)	2925	Jul 98	*Phocea*
Fastnet (biennial race)	605	Aug 99	*Fujicolor II*
Sydney – Hobart (annual race)	630	Dec 99	*Nokia*
Hong Kong – Hainan I, China	330	Jan 00	*Beau Geste*
Brisbane – Gladstone	309	Apr 82	*Shotover*
Sydney – Gold Coast	386	Aug 99	*Brindabella*
San Francisco – Kaneohe, Hawaii, (Pacific Cup, biennial)	2150	Jul 98	*Pyewacket*
Punta del Este – Fremantle (Whitbread)	7875	Nov 93	*Intrum Justitia (European)*
La Baule – Dakar	3500	Oct 87	*Lada-Poch II*
Sydney – Gold Coast	386	Sep 97	*Foxtel Amazon*
Plymouth – Newport two-handed transatlantic E to W	2800	Jun 94	*Primagaz*
St Malo – Guadeloupe (Route du Rhum, quadrennial)	3700	Nov 98	*Primagaz*
Fort Lauderdale – Southampton	3818	May 94	*Tokio*
Los Angeles – Honolulu (Transpac, biennial)	2224	Jul 99	*Pyewacket*
Transpacific, Los Angeles – Honolulu, monohull	2224	Jul 97	*Pyewacket*
Round the Isle of Wight, monohull (rule 5c)	50	Jun 01	*Leopard*
Miami – Montego Bay	811	Feb 99	*Lakota*
Heligoland – Kiel	520	Jul 00	*Uca*
Auckland – Punta del Este (WRTWR)	5914	Feb–Mar 94	*New Zealand Endeavour*
Round the World, Whitbread course, 5 stops	32939	Sep 93–Jun 94	*New Zealand Endeavour*
Fastnet (monohull)	605	Aug 99	*RF Yachting*
Chicago – Mackinac, monohull	293	Jul 87	*Pied Piper*
Cape Town – Rio Race	3435	Jan 00	*Zephyrus IV*
Cape Town – Sydney (BOC Race)	6698	Dec 94	*Sceta Calberson*
San Francisco – Hawaii (singlehanded transpac)	2120	Jul 98	*Lakota*
Puerto Rico, Gran Canaria – Bridgetown, Barbados	2615	Jun 95	*Meril Cup*
Newport RI – Bermuda (biennial race)	635	Jun 96	*Boomerang*
Annapolis – Newport, RI (biennial race)	473	Jun 01	*Carrera*

Correct in late 2001. Faster times may gradually amend the listings, but overall scheme will remain.

Type	LOA ft / m		Owner/Skipper	Nationality	Elapsed Time	Average Speed Kn
C	60	18.29	Steve Fossett	USA	6h 46m 40s	18.45
T	60	18.29	Steve Fossett	USA	2d 14h 20m	15.90
T	60	18.29	Rodney Pattisson & Francis Joyon	FRA/GBR	3h 10m 11s	15.77
C	110	33.53	Grant Dalton	NZ/FRA	62d 6h 56m 33s	15.58
C	60	18.29	Steve Fossett	USA	18h 50m 32s	15.55
T	60	18.29	Loïck Peyron	FRA	7d 20h 24m 43s	15.30
S	244	74.37	Bernard Tapie	FRA	8d 3h 29m	14.96
T	60	18.29	Loïck Peyron	FRA	1d 16h 27m 0s	14.96
S	64	19.51	Stephan Myralf	DEN/AUS	1d 19h 48m 2s	14.38
S	64	19.51	Karl Kwok	HKG	23h 13m 32s	14.21
C	60	18.29	Adrian Rogers	AUS	21h 21m 4s	14.05
IMS	80	24.38	George Snow	AUS	1d 3h 35m 3s	14.00
IMS	70	21.34	Roy Disney	USA	6d 14h 23m	13.57
S	64	19.50	Lawrie Smith	GBR	25d 14h 39m 6s	13.00
T	75	22.86	Loïck Peyron	FRA	11d 9h 19m	12.81
IMS	66	20.12	Peter Walker	AUS	1d 6h 22m 8s	12.71
T	60	18.29	Laurent Bourgnon & Cam Lewis	FRA	9d 8h 5m 20s	12.49
T (I)	60	18.29	Laurent Bourgnon	FRA	12d 8h 41m 6s	12.47
S	64	19.50	Chris Dickson	NZL	12d 19h 37m 48s	12.41
IMS	73	22.25	Roy Disney	USA	7d 11h 41m 27s	12.38
ULDB	70	21.34	Roy Disney	USA	7d 15h 24m 40s	12.13
S	92	28	Mike Slade	GBR	4h 8m 55s	12.05
T	60	18.29	Steve Fossett	USA	2d 20h 8m 5s	11.90
S	67	20.42	Walter Meyer-Kothe	GER	1d 19h 46m 5s	11.88
IOR	85	25.91	Grant Dalton	NZL	21d 2h 26m 13s	11.68
IOR	85	25.91	Grant Dalton	NZL	120d 5h 9m 23s	11.41
S	80	24.38	Ross Field	NZL	2d 5h 8m 51s	11.38
IOR	67	18.29	Dick Jennings	USA	1d 1h 50m 44s	11.33
ULDB	75	22.86	Bob McNeill	USA	12d 16h 49m	11.27
S (I)	60	18.29	Christophe Auguin	FRA	24d 23h 40m 16s	11.17
T (I)	60	18.29	Steve Fossett	USA	7d 22h 38m 26s	11.12
IOR	85	25.91	Pierre Fehlmann	SUI	9d 20h 51m 32s	11.04
IMS	78	23.77	George Coumanataros	USA	2d 9h 31m 50s	11.04
IMS	60	18.29	Joseph Dockery	USA	1d 18h 58m 12s	11.01

Race/Route	Distance Nm	Date	Yacht
Cowes – St Malo (race)	152	Jul 99	*Spirit of England*
Lorient – Bermuda – Lorient	5800	Jun 83	*Charentes Maritime*
La Baule – Dakar	3075	Nov 91	*RMO*
Long Beach – Cabo San Lucas	804	Nov 95	*Lakota*
Miami – Montego Bay, monohull	811	Mar 71	*Windward Passage*
Punta del Este – Newport (BOC)	6000	Apr 91	*Group Sceta*
Victoria (Canada) – Maui, Hawaii	2308	Jul 00	*Grand Illusion*
Buenos Aires – Rio de Janeiro	1200	Feb 87	*Cisne Branco*
Round Britain and Ireland, all islands (race, 4 stops)	1950	Jul 89	*Saab Turbo*
Giraglia	250	Jul 98	*Riviera di Rimini*
Salinas (Ecuador) Baltra	575	Oct 93	*Amnesia*
Punta del Este – Fort Lauderdale (WRTWR)	5475	Apr 94	*Yamaha*
Cowes – St Malo (monohull)	152	Jul 99	*Silk Cut*
Solent – Punta del Este (WRTWR)	5938	Sep-Oct 93	*New Zealand Endeavour*
St Petersburg – Fort Lauderdale	397	Feb 84	*Windward Passage*
Melbourne – Hobart	408	Jan 91	*Wild Thing*
Bayview Port Huron – Mackinac	259	Jul 93	*Windquest*
Sydney – Punta del Este (BOC Race)	7200	Mar 91	*Generali Concorde*
New York – San Francisco (via Cape Horn, Gold Race)	13208	Jan-Mar 98	*Aquitaine Innovations*
Middle Sea race, Malta – Malta	612	Oct 00	*Zephyrus IV*
Le Havre – Cartagena, Colombia (Jacques Vabre monohull)	4419	Nov 99	*Sodebo*
Swiftsure Lightship Classic (Vancouver)	136	May 97	*Stars and Stripes*
Round the World, 4 stops, Newport – Newport, RI (BOC)	7200	Sep 90-Apr 91	*Group Sceta*
San Diego – Manzanillo	1100	Jul 94	*Pyewacket*
Sydney – New Plymouth, NZ (Trans Tasman Double Handed)	1200	Mar 98	*Jarkan*
Daytona, Florida – Bermuda	875	May 91	*Challenge America*
Japan – Guam	1300	Dec 88	*Marishiten*
Los Angeles – Tahiti	3600	Jun 64	*Ticonderoga*
Brisbane – Nouméa (New Caledonia)	823	Sep 97	*Orsa Maggiore*
Melbourne – Osaka (2-handed)	5480	Mar 95	*Wild Thing*
Round the Islands of Hawaii	778	Aug 84	*Boomerang*
Charleston, SC – Cape Town	6851	Oct 98	*Team Group 4*
Bermuda – Plymouth	2870	Aug 74	*Pen Duick VI*
Annapolis – Bermuda	753	Jun 00	*Donnybrook*
Swiftsure lightship classic (Vancouver) monohull	136	May 95	*Cassiopeia*
Auckland – Fiji – Guam – Fukuoka	5500	Apr 89	*Tobiume*
Los Angeles – Osaka (Pan Pac Race)	5297	Jun 94	*North West Spirit*
Round Australia	6500	Oct 99	*Magna Data*

Type	LOA ft/m		Owner/Skipper	Nationality	Elapsed Time	Average Speed Kn
T	43	13.11	Peter Clutterbuck	GBR	13h 50m 20s	10.98
C	66	21.42	Pierre Follenfant	FRA	22d 9h 1m 45s	10.80
T (I)	60	18.29	Laurent Bourgnon	FRA	11d 22h 41m 32s	10.73
T	60	18.29	Steve Fossett	USA	3d 2h 59m 49s	10.72
CCA	73	22.25	Mark Johnson	USA	3d 3h 40m	10.70
S (I)	60	18.29	Christophe Auguin	FRA	23d 14h 11m 22s	10.60
ULDB	70	21.34	James McDowell	USA	9d 2h 8m 27s	10.58
IOR	80	24.40	F A Rocha Coelho	BRA	4d 18h 52m 57s	10.44
C	75	22.86	François Boucher	FRA	7d 7h 30m	10.40
S	55	16.7	Paolo Cian	ITA	1d 0h 11m 28s	10.34
S	64	19.50	Estefano Isiase S Salam	ECU	2d 7h	10.29
S	64	19.50	Ross Field	NZL	22d 5h 13m 50s	10.26
S	64	19.50	Lawrie Smith	GBR	14h 48m 15s	10.25
IOR	85	25.91	Grant Dalton	NZL	24d 7h 19m 2s	10.18
IOR	73	22.25	John Rumsey	USA	1d 15h 15m	10.10
IOR	47	14.33	Grant Wharington	AUS	2d 0h 20m 19s	9.93
IMS	70	21.34	Rich & Doug Devos	USA	1d 8h 13m 1s	9.70
S (I)	60	18.29	Alain Gautier	FRA	31d 3h 21m 14s	9.63
S	60	18.29	Yves Parlier	FRA	57d 3h 21m 45s	9.63
ULDB	75	22.86	Bob McNeil	USA	2d 16h 49m 57s	9.44
S	60	18.29	Thomas Coville & Hervé Jan	FRA	19d 17h 31m	9.33
C	60	18.29	Steve Fossett	USA	14h 35m 29s	9.32
S (I)	60	18.29	Christophe Auguin	FRA	120d 22h 36m 35s	9.30
IMS	80	24.38	Roy Disney	USA	5d 0h 17m	9.14
S	60	18.29	Kanga Birtles	AUS	5d 16h 36m	8.80
IOR	80	24.38	Teddy Turner	USA	4d 3h 50m 19s	8.76
ULDB	68	20.00	Hirosugu-Hash	JPN	6d 4h 10m	8.70
CCA	72	21.94	Bob Johnson	USA	17d 7h 58m	8.65
S	98	30	Armando Leoni	ITA	3d 23h 40m 26s	8.60
S	50	15.1	Grant Wharington	AUS	26d 20h 47m 6s	8.50
IOR	81	24.69	Jeff Neuthberg	USA	3d 22h 35m	8.23
S (I)	60	18.29	Mike Golding	GBR	34d 18h 54m	8.21
IOR	74	22.55	Eric Tabarly	FRA	14d 20h 15m 12s	8.20
S	72	22.03	James Muldoon	USA	4d 0h 50m 34s	7.78
IMS	72	21.94	C Burnett & C Booth	USA	17h 52m 32s	7.61
IOR	48	14.3	Tadatoshi Saita	JPN	30d 3h 8m	7.60
S	60	18.29	John Oman	USA	32d 16h 2m 36s	6.75
S	60	18.29	Jeremy Pearce	AUS	43d 19h 29m 55s	6.18

Index of subjects

500-metre run, creation of 24
  future projects 00
  venues 35
40-knot Sailboat 19
America's Cup facts 107
American east coast races 63
Argos device 96
Atlantic routes 61
attempts still possible 121
Australasian routes 61

board sailing speeds 29
Brenton Reef Cup 12
Britain and Ireland, around 65,
  126
  power 118

chronology of records 104
Cowes to Dinard/St Malo 67

day's record run 94

English Channel routes 66

Fastest sailors, current 32
Fastnet race 68, 125
'Firsts' 102

Fourteen Foot International 16
Fox, Uffa 16, 18

'Gold Route' (New York to San
  Francisco) 58, 123

Golden Globe race 80
'great capes' 77, 80
Guinness Book of Records 2, 38

Harmsworth Trophy 116

ice yachts 113
IMCO 4
International Canoe class 18
ISAF (International Sailing
  Federation) 4, 52
Isle of Wight, around 67, 126

J-class 12, 14

Land yachts 113

Mediterranean routes 60, 125
Millennium Race ('The Race') 62,
  93
motor boat speeds 114

New York–Lizard 51, 124
Newport, CA–Ensenada 59
Newport, RI–Bermuda 63, 124

ocean racing 1974 records 44
offshore rules 41
oldest sailors 103
one-designs, earliest 106
ORC 38
OSTAR 43, 54, 65, 79

Pacific Ocean routes 57
Plymouth–Newport, RI 21,97
Portland Speed Week 26,28
power boats 115

Round Britain and Ireland race 22
Royal Cork Yacht Club 115
Royal Cruising Club 103
Royal Ocean Racing Club 65
Royal Yacht Squadron 5
Royal Yachting Association 24

Sandy Hook area 54
Search for Speed Under Sail 7
smallest boat 108
speed criteria 15
speed/length ratio 6
speed trials, early 23
starters in race record 106
Sunday Times sponsorship 48

Tornado class 23
trade wind races 62

transatlantic race beginnings 46
Transpac route 58–9

UIM (Union Internationale
    Motonautique) 4
Universal rule 14
US Navy 19

Vendée Globe 52, 77, 83, 88, 122
Verne, Jules 90, 93

Westabout around the world races
    90
Whitbread race 81
women around the world 84
world, around in 80 days 90
    routes 74
    rules 77
    early voyages 78

youngest sailors 103
Yachting World speed trials 23
yacht club records 111

Index of boats and people

Adelaide 9
Aikane 22
America 5, 9, 45, 67
American Eagle 70
American Promise 37, 87
Aquitaine Innovations 57
Armor Lux 52, 54, 101
Arthaud, Florence 60
Atlantic 46, 47, 48, 49, 50, 54
Autissier, Isabelle 58
Avenger 16

Bagages Supérior 88
Baker, J G 19
Bielak, Thierry 32
Blake, Peter 91
Blyth, Chay 22, 57, 81, 90
Boomerang 63
Bradfield, 'Brad' 30
Britannia 10, 11, 12
British Steel 81, 90
Brynhild 17

Cable & Wireless Adventurer 119
Calluna 10
Caradec, Loïck 22
Champion of the Seas 7, 94
Chichester, Francis 44, 74, 77, 79, 80, 102
Choy, Rudy 21
Clarke, 'Nobby' 38
Clifton Flasher 29
ClubMed 62, 93, 100, 110

Cohoe 48
Colas, Alain 21
Colman, Tim 26, 27
Colonia 10
Commodore Explorer 91
Cooke, Brian 22
Cottee, Kay 88
Crédit Agricole 83
Crossbow 26, 27, 28, 30
Crossbow II 27, 28, 30, 31
Cunningham, Lindsay 32
Cutty Sark 9

Dauntless 10
Dazzler 65
Desjoyeaux, Michel 88
Desperado 48
Dexia Eure et Loire 68
Disney, Roy 59
Donald McKay 7
Dorade 43, 48
Ecureuil d'Aquitaine 88
Edwards, Tracy 54, 86
Elf Aquitaine 49
Endeavour (cat) 23
Endeavour (J) 14
English Rose V 87
Enza 91
Experiment 20

Field, Ross 72
Fila 52
Fleury Michon 45, 54, 95, 97

Flying Cloud 8, 57
Folatre 21
Formule Tag 95
Fossett, Steve 59, 60, 67, 93
    achievements of 64, 68
Fujicolor II 72

Gallant 17, 18
Geodis 52
Gipsy Moth III 44
Gipsy Moth IV 74, 79, 80
Gipsy Moth V 83
Golding, Mike 90
Great Britain II 81, 82
Great Britain III 48
Great Britain IV (tri) 22
Grogono, James 26
Guinevere 10

Hansford, Philip 29
Hasler, 'Blondie' 43
Helsal 44, 61
Herreshoff, Nathanael 20
Humphreys, Rob 90

Icarus 26
Icicle 114

Jacob's Ladder 29
James Baines 7, 9
James, Rob 22
Jeantot, Philippe 87
Jet Services V 49, 51
Jolie Brise 68, 72
Jubilee 10

Kelsall, Derek 21, 22, 65
Kersauson, Olivier de 48, 91
Kialoa II 48
Kingfisher 86
Knox-Johnston, Robin 66, 74, 75,

    80, 91, 107
Kriter Brut de Brut 37
Kriter IV 48
Kriter VIII 50

Lady Helmsman 23
Lakota 60, 64, 65, 66
Lamazou, Titouan 88, 90
Lightning 7, 8, 94
Longshot 30, 35

Macalpine-Downie, Rod 26
MacArthur, Ellen 86, 88
Maka, Pascal 30, 31, 32
Manureva 21, 82
Mari-Cha III 52, 54, 61
Mayfly 29
McKay, Donald 7
McMullen, Mike 22
Monitor 19
Monnet, Philippe 37, 58, 90

Navahoe 10, 12
Nicol, Hedley 21
Nicorette 51
Nina 68
Nirvana 70
Nordwind 70
Northern Light 107
Ondine 44, 48

Pajot, Marc 49
Parlier, Yves 57
Parry Endeavour 92
Patriarch 82
Pattisson, Rodney 26, 68
Paul Ricard 49
Pelly, David 26
Pen Duick II 44
Pen Duick IV 21
Pen Duick VI 44

Perie Banou 91
Petty, Sir William 20
Peyron, Bruno 59, 91, 93
Peyron, Loïck 72, 93
Pilgrim 10
Piver, Arthur 21
PlayStation 63, 67, 97, 101
Preussen 8
Primagaz 53, 54, 97
Pucher, Michael 30
Puritan 7
Pyewacket 59

Ranger 12, 14
Reliance 107
RF Yachting 72
Royal & Sun Alliance 54, 86

Saab Turbo 65
Sail That Dream 65
Samuel Pepys 48
Sanders, Jon 91
Satanita 10, 11, 12
Sayula 81
Scott, Peter 23, 24
Shadow 48
Shamrock 14
Silk Cut 98

Slocum, Joshua 73
Sparkman & Stephens 43
Spirit of Australia 116
Sport Elec 91
Spray 73
Stamm, Bernard 101
Stars and Stripes 59, 63
Suhaili 74, 75, 80, 81, 107, 108

Tabarly, Eric 21
Team Pindar 65
Thermopylae 9
Thomas, David 90
Toria 21, 65
Triton (USS) 74, 119

Uunet 90

Valkyrie II 10
Velsheda 14
Vigilant 10

Waikiki Surf 21
Winston 51

Yellow Pages 25, 33, 35

Zeal 65